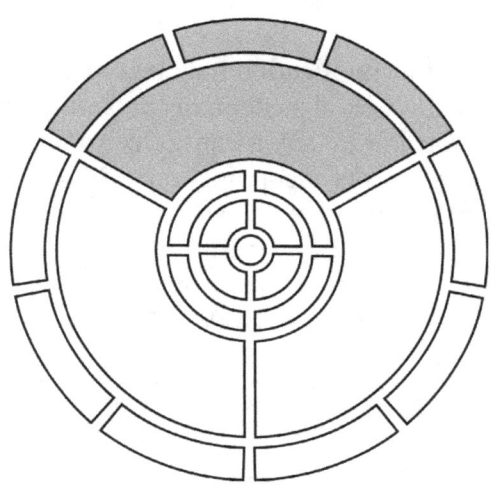

STRATEGY & ALIGNMENT

How the Most Successful Leaders Analyze Needs,
Prioritize, Craft Vision, Align Stakeholders and
Create Smart Strategic Plans

First Print Edition, February 2025

Copyright © 2023-2025 Brett Thomas and Integral Publishing, LLC

No part of this publication may be reproduced, stored in a retrieval system, or transmitted in any form or by any means, electronic, mechanical, photocopying, recording, or otherwise, without written permission of the publisher.

ISBN 9798310037076

Published by Integral Publishing, LLC

Printed in the U.S.A.

First published November 2023
First print version February 2025

CONTENTS

INTRODUCTION 1

CHAPTER 1: WHY MOST LEADERSHIP DEVELOPMENT EFFORTS FAIL 3

CHAPTER 2: THE LEADERSHIP ROSETTA STONE 19

CHAPTER 3: THE UNIVERSAL LEADERSHIP MODEL 33

CHAPTER 4: THE INTEGRAL LEADERSHIP METHODOLOGY 53

CHAPTER 5: BENCHMARKING THE STRATEGY & ALIGNMENT LEADERSHIP CAPACITY 115

CHAPTER 6: SENSEMAKING 127

CHAPTER 7: STAKEHOLDER ALIGNMENT 163

CHAPTER 8: DYNAMIC STEERING 193

CONCLUSION: WHERE TO GO FROM HERE ON YOUR LEADERSHIP JOURNEY 221

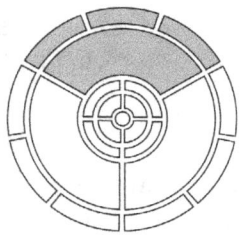

INTRODUCTION

This book introduces you to a major breakthrough in the field of leadership and leadership development. In a field where most so-called "experts" cannot even agree on a single definition of leadership, and the vast majority of leadership development programs fail, many of my clients and readers appreciate the clarity that this *Integral Leadership* book series brings to a confusing and often overwhelming topic. *Strategy & Alignment* is the next groundbreaking book on rapid leadership development in this series. This book provides detailed practices, techniques and leadership skills that help managers and executives make sense out of their external and internal environment, analyze organizational needs, prioritize opportunities and projects, craft a compelling vision, align their stakeholders and garner their commitment, solve problems, make effective decisions and create smart, evolving strategic plans that help them successfully steer their organization quarter by quarter, year by year to the "destination" described in their vision. Unlike most books on leadership that focus on abstract concepts and vague "leadership qualities," this book drills right down into specific, tangible techniques that amount to the exact behaviors that make leaders successful in this crucial dimension of leadership.

This book also presents a compelling argument as to why the "bogus" leadership development industry is not truly developing leaders. It introduces the world's first "Unifying Theory of Leadership" and reveals my 20-year "trade secret" on how we consistently achieve outstanding results with our leadership development programs (in an industry where that generally produces lackluster results).

> *The approach to leadership and leadership development outlined in this book is almost certainly unlike anything you've ever seen before. Most leadership trainings and many books about leadership fail to define the specific abilities, skill sets, techniques and behaviors that make up the complex skill called leadership. In fact, most so-called leadership experts don't even recognize that leadership is a complex skill.*

This book is the remedy for that. The information contained within is based on over 20 years of experience advising leaders, training leaders, and coaching leaders and executive teams.

My experience avails me a unique perspective about which methods actually produce improvements in leadership skills, as opposed to those that only increase a leader's knowledge of concepts but do little to change their behavior.

I am approaching this book as a conversation with you, the reader. I am assuming that in your role of leader, you already are familiar with many aspects of leadership (and leadership development). If you find this "conversation" valuable, I hope we can continue the conversation in my other books that unpack and expand upon the ideas introduced here. I expect that this will be one of the most valuable books you've ever read on leadership.

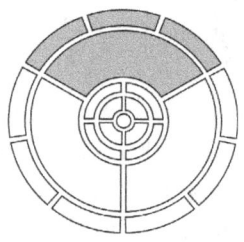

CHAPTER 1:
WHY MOST LEADERSHIP DEVELOPMENT EFFORTS FAIL

Many studies from best-in-class organizations, institutions and publications in recent years have drawn the same conclusion: most leadership development efforts fail. This is no exaggeration, this is simply a matter of fact that is easily verified. Numerous studies from prominent institutions estimate that approximately .70 to .80 cents of every dollar spent on leadership development is wasted. I have personally reviewed numerous studies that back up this assertion. I have devoted my professional career to this field of leadership development and it has been of great interest to me to stay on top of the current industry practices and compare my unique methodology to what my peers and competitors are doing. I am very familiar with how leadership training and coaching is typically done (and how it is very slowly evolving). Most leadership training programs amount to one and two week classroom seminars with lectures about leadership character traits, leader qualities, or abstract concepts that have little bearing on learning the actual concrete techniques (behaviors) that can improve leadership performance.

I'm sure you have come into contact with this problem. When you try to read books, attend leadership seminars or speak to executive coaches, it seems that they all have a different idea of what constitutes effective leadership, and their ideas largely contradict each other.

Bernard Bass, the well-respected leadership researcher and author of *The Bass Handbook of Leadership: Theory and Managerial Applications,* has noted, "Any two-day conference on leadership begins with one day of argumentation about what leadership means."

Many business professors, when speaking candidly, admit this fact that no one can agree on a definition or description of effective leadership. MIT Sloan management professor John Van Maanen has stated, "Even today, three-plus decades in, there's no real definition of it."

William Deresiewicz, the author of the book, *Excellent Sheep,* points out while every college in the country claims to be producing leaders, no one appears to know what the word even means. "There seem to be two possibilities," he writes, "The first is that it means nothing at all, or whatever definition is useful at any given time. The second is that it simply means being in charge."

Another well-known theorist, Fred Fiedler, observed, "There are almost as many definitions of leadership as there are leadership theories—and there are almost as many theories of leadership as there are psychologists working in the field."

The reason why there is almost no agreement among leadership advice givers on a single definition of "effective leadership" is that each different "type" of follower and leadership advice giver looks for different qualities and behaviors in what they consider to be "effective leaders".

This is because all followers and all advice-givers have one of our different worldviews. I will introduce these worldviews as a central part of my model in later chapters.

Here, I will mention that leadership advice is often bogus because instead of *one* definition of effective leadership, there are actually *four* definitions. Each of the four camps of advice givers has its own definition of effective leadership, which essentially amounts to them using their definition of "effective leadership" to push their own unconscious bias. The field of leadership theory and leadership development is riddled with unconscious bias and represents one of the biggest reasons so much of it is so bogus.

Few, if any, contextualize their definition of effective leadership by saying, this is a definition of effective leadership for "traditional types" or for "postmodern" or "progressive" types. Rather, they just push their unconscious bias and suggest their definition of effective leadership (for one of the worldviews) as the most effective way to lead all four types of followers. This is, of course, untrue, but that doesn't stop them from saying it.

It is no exaggeration to say that the advice givers in the leadership industry have failed to provide a definition or description of effective leadership that they can agree to.

Barbara Kellerman, a Harvard professor, takes it one step further when she says the leadership industry has failed. She explains, "The leadership industry has failed over its roughly 40 year history to improve the human condition in any major, meaningful, measurable way."

She is one of the few honest leadership professors who doesn't pull punches. Kellerman is a distinguished professor at Harvard University's John F. Kennedy School of Government. She was the Founding Executive Director at Harvard's Kennedy School's Center for Public Leadership, and previously served as the Director of the Center for the Advanced Study of Leadership at the Academy of Leadership at the University of Maryland. Kellerman has written a series of books that amount to scathing take downs of the bogus leadership industry including: *Bad Leadership, The End of Leadership,* and *Professionalizing Leadership.*

In *The End of Leadership,* she describes how despite the countless leadership programs, courses, seminars, trainers, consultants and coaches claiming to teach people how to lead, there is "scant evidence" that this enormous investment of time and money has paid off. (The leadership development industry is estimated to be $15 billion annually in the U.S. and $50 billion worldwide.)

In her follow up book, *Professionalizing Leadership,* she notes that since the publishing of the End of Leadership in 2012, she is no longer alone in beginning to blow the whistle on these unethical practices such as trying to teach a complex and technical skill in a two-week seminar (which is what most of them do). "Since then, I have been joined by a small but fierce cadre of others who point to the yawning gap between what the leadership industry claims to do, and what it does."

Kellerman is joined by Stanford's Jeffrey Pfeffer as respected academics, thoughtful intellectuals, and true insiders who have recently turned leadership industry "whistleblowers."

Pfeffer, a prominent Stanford business school professor, and author of numerous books on management and leadership, including *Leadership BS: Fixing Workplaces and Careers One Truth at a Time,* writes "The single biggest barrier to effective leadership is, in my view, the leadership industry itself. Instead of telling people the skills and behaviors they need to be effective in getting things done, we tell them almost the opposite—blandishments about how we wish people would be, and how we wish workplaces were."

He states flatly "The leadership industry has failed. It's not just that all the efforts to develop better leaders have failed to appreciably improve leadership, but they often make things much worse."

Pfeffer writes, "If one is at all sensitive to the human costs incurred as leaders flame out and lose their jobs, cares and concerns that I and I suspect many others share, then the continuing failure of the leadership industry in all of its forms and activities to make things better needs to be both explained and remedied."

Finally, leadership researcher and New York Times bestselling author Duff McDonald describes the leadership industry this way, "Most of it is bullshit. Unfortunately, there are few business school faculty who could ever summon the courage to admit such a thing. But some do, and using the same language."

For our purposes here, I want to highlight three crucial facts in this whole sordid affair that is the leadership training and coaching industry.

First, the vast majority of so-called leadership experts, trainers and coaches do not know the answers to the most basic questions about leadership: what is leadership, how does it work, and how can you develop it?

Second, as I explained above, none of the leadership experts can agree on which approach or style works best. In fact, about 90% of experts will tell you that the style they advocate is the "best" style and should pretty much be used with all people and circumstances.

Finally, as I mentioned already and will explain in more detail later in this book, the reason that the experts can't agree on the above fundamentals is because they are "subject to their own worldview bias." I will explain this in more detail later, but this essentially, it means that they are unaware of their assumptions and biases about human psychology, human motivation, and follower's needs and behavior.

My colleagues and I, under the guidance of my mentor Ken Wilber, were the first to notice (and teach and write about) this pattern. This pattern, definitively explains why there are so many definitions and descriptions of "effective" leadership that wildly contradict each other to the point of being often mutually exclusive.

This is why, as you will see shortly, worldviews are right at the center of my model. And the different leadership approaches (or styles as they can be called) that each of the four worldviews expects from legitimate and credible leaders (in their eyes) is also at the center of my model. This is what makes it universal.

Rather than a one-size-fits-all approach that amounts to pushing one's unconscious worldview bias, the new approach described in this book accounts for different follower worldviews, needs and preferences, and accounts for the four universal leadership styles seen in nearly all leadership theory literature and leadership research.

My "Universal Leadership Model," explained in detail in a later chapter, is the first model that connects these four universal worldviews with the four universal leadership styles. This connection forms the heart of the " Unifying Theory of Leadership" that I developed with Ken Wilber at the Integral Institute.

This "meta theory" of leadership explains which leadership approach (or style) will work with which people and circumstances, and what approaches will be disastrous with which people and circumstances.

My *Practice-based Leadership Development* methodology, which I will explain in detail in a later chapter, is also unique in that it is the first to break down the technical and complex skill of leadership into three "essential abilities" and nine essential leadership practices, and then proceeds to train leaders using "Deliberate Practice" which comes from the field of Expert Performance Theory, developed by Anders Ericsson.

In the next chapter, *The Leadership Rosetta Stone,* I outline the four different definitions of "effective leadership" that the four different camps of leadership advice- givers offer (which reflect their unconscious worldview bias).

For now, it is useful to offer a stripped down, you could say generic or "worldview agnostic" definition, free of worldview bias.

> *Leadership: the ability or activity of inspiring and/or influencing people in relationship, over time, toward shared goals.*

The word "leadership" implies a trust-based relationship over time with shared goals, and the word "follower" implies voluntary (consensual) participation. Remember that followership is voluntary. A follower chooses to see a person as their leader, and that can be revoked (by the follower) at any time. A follower offers discretionary effort, that is effort above and beyond what would be considered compliance, in the case of an authority figure compelling them to comply with their order.

So when influence occurs within the context of a leader-follower relationship, the follower is voluntarily participating in being influenced. Put another way, followers actually want the leader to influence them. Followers give the leader consent to influence them.

Bringing all of this together, we can think of "leadership influence" as *affecting a follower in such a way that they voluntarily change how they think or behave.*

The next big idea I want to highlight in this introduction lies at the very heart of why 80% of leadership development efforts fail, and why so much of leadership theory and so much leadership advice, is so utterly bogus.

This may strike you as a little bit provocative, controversial, or, in the worst case even condescending. But it's really none of those things if you hear me out and grasp the nuance of the reality that I'm pointing out for you.

So, bear with me and you will be glad that you did. Many leadership trainers and coaches talk about leadership as if it is about personality traits, or qualities, or vague concepts like EQ (more on this later). While these topics are interesting in the background, discussing them does next to nothing to help leaders actually improve their leadership performance.

Many leadership trainers and coaches talk about leadership as if it is about personality traits, or qualities or vague concepts like EQ (more on this later). While these topics are interesting in the background, discussing them does next to nothing to help leaders actually improve their leadership performance. Improving leadership performance has little to do with concepts and everything to do with skill. The vast majority of leadership trainers and coaches seem to be ignorant of the relatively obvious and definitely indisputable fact that leadership is a technical and complex skill.

> *There is only one way to learn a technical and / or complex skill. That is to train in the specific, requisite techniques until they are internalized as habits, then layer on more techniques to create skills, then combine several new skills to create new "skill sets" and ultimately those skill sets mature into what we call "abilities."*

This crucial point is a central element in my rapid leadership development methodology called "Accelerating Leadership," that is the subject of Chapter 4. To get better at leadership, you must understand the nature of leadership. Leadership is not a set of personality traits and it is not some vague concept (although many authors, trainers and coaches speak about it as though it is).

> *Leadership is a technical and complex skill, no different from all the many other technical and complex skills you have already learned both as a child and as an adult.*

You know this intuitively, but for some odd reason, most leadership authors, trainers and coaches don't seem to.

Learning the technical and complex skill of leadership is no different than learning any of those other technical and complex skills that you already taken the time to learn. The method is exactly the same. Yet less than 10% of leadership development programs use it.

Learning leadership is exactly the same as learning to play a musical instrument, mastering a martial art or sport, flying an airplane or any other technical and/or complex skill. How could it be otherwise?

To "reinvent leadership" we must first face the stark reality that leadership, like every other technical and complex skill we have already learned in our lives, is comprised of skills and those skills are, in turn, comprised of techniques (that can also be referred to as "practices").

Any proposed explanation of leadership that fails to point to the techniques and practices that comprise the technical and complex skill called "leadership" is flawed from the start. And this is why about 90% of models, frameworks and explanations offered by leadership advice-givers are bogus.

This is such an important point, I am going to revisit it several times in this book coming at it from a variety of different angles and using different analogies. Please pardon my deliberate repetition, but if there is one thing you must understand, it is this. And I don't want you to just be familiar with it as a concept, I want you to believe it and understand it in your bones. Once you do, all of your future leadership development efforts (and the efforts in your organization) will be much easier and more effective. This is one of the main things I want you to get out of this book.

Let me illustrate this crucial point in very concrete terms that I hope you can relate to on a personal level. I will refer to several other common technical and complex skills that you may have already learned.

Learning Guitar

No one in their right mind would try to learn to play an instrument, try to learn a martial art, or try to learn to fly an airplane the way 90% of leadership development programs train leadership. Can you imagine trying to learn to play the guitar by reading case studies of great guitar players in history, or worse, hearing stories about the accomplishments of great guitarists, or worse still, reading a list of character traits of these men and women?

Learning a Martial Art

Can you imagine trying to learn Kung Fu by hearing stories about Bruce Lee, and descriptions of his personality traits or by merely adopting his mindset or philosophy?

As absurd as this sounds, it is even more absurd that this is exactly what approximately 90% of leadership development programs are doing in the $15 billion-a-year leadership development industry (in the United States alone).

My team and I have been creating and delivering successful leadership development programs for over two decades, and I am now calling out these bogus industry practices. Research shows clearly that programs that emphasize leadership qualities, traits, philosophy, and case studies (instead of techniques and practices) fail to help leaders improve their leadership skills or their leadership performance.

Learning Piano

I want you to pause for a moment and imagine signing up your son or daughter to a training to learn to play piano and asking them what techniques your child will be practicing each week. Now imagine that their answer is, "Our students don't practice any specific techniques. Our students study the stories and personality traits of great piano players."

There is an entire field called "Complex Skill Instructional Design." Google it.

It is a very well-known fact in training and development that in order to learn any technical or complex skill, you must break the overall ability down into specific skill sets and skills, and then down to the techniques that make up those skills.

This is common sense. You already know this.

Sports Such as Baseball or Basketball

Consider the technical and complex skill called baseball. Many children learn this complex skill. Perhaps you did. When you (or your child, niece or nephew) learned the ability to play baseball, it was broken down to *throwing, catching, hitting the ball, and running the bases*. In the case of basketball, it is *dribbling, passing, shooting* and *rebounding*. In the case of mixed martial arts, it is *wrestling, kick-boxing* and *grappling*.

There is also a well-known field called "Expert Performance Theory" or "Deliberate Practice" (as it is better known). You have no doubt heard of "10,000 hours" as the estimated amount of time it takes for a person practicing deliberately to go from beginner to expert level in any complex skill.

Why don't leadership development programs incorporate "Deliberate Practice" into their efforts and teach their students the practices (the techniques and skills) that leaders need to be effective?

My partners, colleagues and I have been teaching the complex skill called "leadership" using "complex skill instructional design" and "deliberate practice" for more than 20 years. I have logged more than 20,000 hours doing precisely that. So, let me save you a lot of time, energy, money and heartburn and tell you what does not work and exactly what does actually work for leadership development.

I summarize what works in this introduction and will unpack each of these ideas in different chapters within the book.

Leadership, like any other complex skill, is made up of a specific set of skills with discrete, concrete behaviors that can be practiced, repeated, and internalized as habits.

Again, using baseball as a familiar example, you have to be able to throw, hit, run, and do several other skills before you have the ability that we call "baseball." The same goes for martial arts, music, flying an airplane and leadership.

There is only one way to learn a complex skill: practice and internalize a technique, then combine several techniques (in layers) over time.

This is called "complex skill instructional design" and "deliberate practice." It involves breaking the broader ability down into smaller skill sets and skills, then teaching those specific techniques and behaviors.

Clearly, to learn (or improve) this ability called leadership, it must be broken down into specific skill sets and discrete techniques (behaviors).

Think about mixed martial arts (MMA). There are three major abilities (*wrestling, striking* and *grappling*) and each is made up of a dozen or so techniques. The fact that MMA athletes have separate training and separate coaches for wrestling, striking and grappling underscores the nature of this complex ability (which has many parallels to leadership, which is obviously at least as complex as martial arts).

I will now summarize why I think the leadership development industry is not developing leaders.

1. Most leadership trainers and coaches do not recognize leadership as a technical and complex skill, and instead, speak about leader character traits (or qualities as they often call them).

2. Most leadership trainers and coaches focus primarily or even exclusively on the leader and under-emphasize or completely ignore the leadership context (the specific circumstances that will call for different approaches).

3. Most leadership trainers and coaches under-emphasize or completely ignore the followers, their worldviews (values, beliefs,

assumptions), their specific needs, and their preferences for the kind of leadership they will resonate with

4. Most leadership advice-givers make "one-size-fits-all" pronouncements that this is the "best way" to lead with all followers in all circumstances. Any leadership advice that fails to provide guidelines for which people and circumstances this method will work with is bad advice because no leadership approach will work with all follower types and in all circumstances.

5. Most leadership advice is based on a very rudimentary and unsophisticated understanding of psychology. Very few advice-givers have a working knowledge of Positive Psychology, Interpersonal Psychology, Developmental Psychology or Integral Psychology—all of which are essential to make sense of such a complex field as organizational leadership.

I can summarize all of this by saying that the vast majority of so-called "leadership experts" in today's leadership development industry do not know what leadership actually is, can't explain to customers how leadership actually works, and certainly do not understand how to develop this complex and technical skill (that they don't even recognize as such).

I will reserve an in-depth analysis of what is badly wrong with the leadership development industry for my book, *Blowing the Whistle on Bogus Leadership: Veteran Industry Insider Reveals Why the Leadership Development Industry is Not Developing Leaders*.

Now that we have discussed what makes so much leadership advice bogus, we will transition into a description of a series of astonishing breakthroughs that have occurred in recent years that will allow us to actually reinvent leadership in the coming years.

The beginning of these breakthroughs occurred in the early 2000s at the Stagen Leadership Academy that I co-founded and at Ken Wilber's Integral Institute (where I was the head of the Business and Leadership Center). After over a million dollars in research and development costs over a ten year period, we ultimately found the key to unlock our elusive "unifying theory of leadership" which revealed the pattern that connects all leadership theories, and explains which leadership approaches will work with which people and circumstances (and which will fail with which people and circumstances). We dubbed the discover "The Leadership Rosetta Stone," the topic of the next chapter.

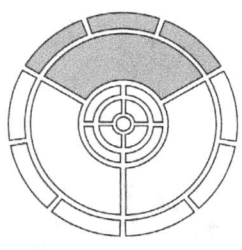

CHAPTER 2: THE LEADERSHIP ROSETTA STONE

The Rosetta Stone is an ancient Egyptian artifact on which the same information is inscribed in: Egyptian hieroglyphs, Demotic, and Greek. The discovery of the Rosetta Stone allowed researchers to decode the language of Egyptian hieroglyphs for the first time in history. This term "Rosetta Stone" is often used idiomatically to describe any critical key that unlocks something previously difficult (or impossible) to decipher.

After reviewing hundreds of leadership texts, including most of the popular books on leadership theory and practice, an unmistakable pattern emerged for me and my research team at The Integral Institute (under the mentorship of Ken Wilber) and the Stagen Leadership Academy. Nearly all "leadership theory" texts and books that claim to explain the "best" way to lead describe the writers' subjective ideas about which leadership tactics work best with followers based on their own assumptions about the world and the people being led. All of the texts that described the authors' opinions about which leadership techniques/approaches work best with followers are based on their assumptions about the world and the people being led.

With rare exceptions, the authors' inherent assumptions about the world and people (and biases for which approaches should be used) lined up with the four "worldviews" I had learned about from Ken Wilber, Jean Gebser, Robert Kegan and the other developmental psychologists I had studied or worked with.

This turned out to be the key to unlocking the Universal Theory of Leadership. When we group the leadership theories, approaches, techniques and tools by the worldview of their advocate, we see that in most cases, those methods do work well for followers who share that worldview. Integral theory provides us with an easy way (if you know what to look for) to identify follower mindsets, or worldviews.

Therefore, if we know a follower's worldview, we will know with a great deal of accuracy which leadership styles and approaches will be most resonant with them, that they will feel drawn to, will trust, willingly follow, and the leader for whom they will happily offer their "discretionary effort."

Next, I will first summarize the four most common worldviews most relevant in organizational life in the developed world and briefly introduce the four universal leadership styles and show how you apply them to the three essential leadership abilities and nine leadership core competencies.

The Four Universal Worldviews

In a later section of this book entitled "Values Research," I will provide a detailed description of decades of values and worldviews research that demonstrates that nearly all major theorists (who study values and worldviews) agree that there are four universal worldviews, and nearly all also agree on their common names). For now, I will keep the discussion brief and simply introduce the Four Universal Worldviews that are essential building blocks for our Leadership Rosetta Stone.

These four worldviews should be familiar to you by now as I introduced them previously when I explained the four leadership paradigms.

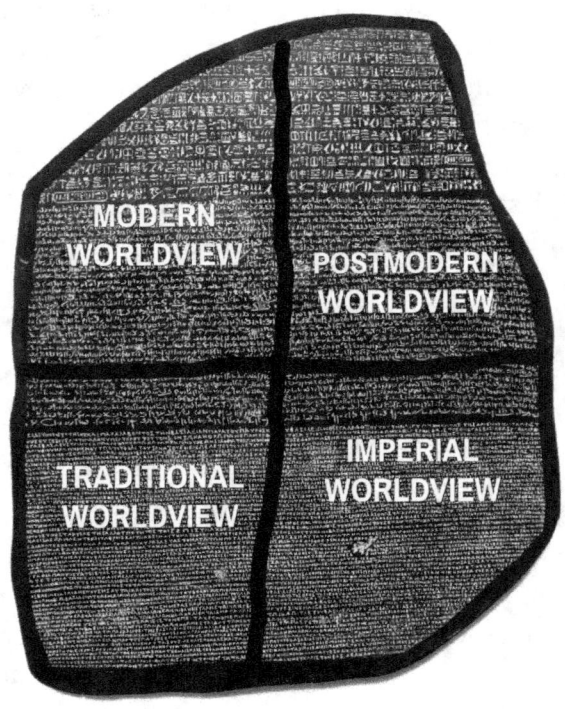

The Imperial Worldview

The Imperial worldview first emerged in society during the time of feudal kingdoms and is roughly equivalent to the Bronze Age and is still very much alive and well today. People with this worldview see the world as made up of "predators and prey", where the strongest and most cunning survive, gain power, and satisfy their wants. They tend to be fiercely independent living by their "own rules" and are disinterested in conforming to many social norms, are driven to break free from limits, achieve their goals, or impose their will. People with this worldview tend to believe the best way to think and behave is "my way." People with an *Imperial* worldview find the *Autocratic* leadership style most credible.

The Traditional Worldview

The Traditional worldview initially emerged historically with the monotheistic religious traditions and the Roman Empire, and we see it starting with the Iron Age (and continuing through the Middle Ages.) People with this worldview see the world as an ordered existence under the control of a higher authority and ultimate truth. They tend to see the world in a concrete, literal, and dualistic manner: right vs. wrong, good vs. evil, and so on. They emphasize social stability and "mainstream" morality. People with this worldview tend to believe that there is only one right way to think and behave. People with a *Traditional* worldview will find the *Bureaucratic* style (also called Authoritarian style) most credible.

The Modern Worldview

The Modern Age emerged during the historical western enlightenment and the dawn of scientific thinking we associate with "The Renaissance", which eventually led to the Industrial Age. People with this worldview tend to believe in the advancement of humankind through the application of the rational mind and its scientific, technological, and medical manifestations. Life is to be met and mastered by finding the best way to act on its limitless opportunities. People with this worldview tend to believe that while there are many valid ways to think and behave, there is always one best way. People with *Modern* worldview will find the *Strategic* leadership style most credible.

The Postmodern Worldview

The Postmodern worldview first emerged in the 1960s with the advent of computer technology, networking and globalization and we associate it with the Information Age. People with this worldview believe the world is a diverse web of interrelationships where life forms depend on each other for survival, and there is no single explanatory system (view of reality) that can account for all the phenomena of life; rather there are many truths. People with this worldview tend to believe that there are many valid ways to think and behave but that there is no real way to judge the superiority of one way or another. People with *Postmodern* worldview will find the *Humanistic* leadership style most credible.

Now that we have initially defined the four worldviews, we will look at the four "universal leadership styles" that must be paired with people who share these corresponding worldviews in order to be viewed as a credible leader in the eyes of your followers.

The Four Universal Leadership Styles

To aid in the learning process, I will first provide a "fly over" with the four very brief definitions and descriptions of the four universal leadership styles that provide a hub that the Universal Leadership Model spins around.

Autocratic Leadership: The person with the most power leads via command and control. In short, this leadership style is based on power and control.

Bureaucratic Leadership: The person with positional authority leads via chain of command. In short, this leadership style is based on rules and compliance.

Strategic Leadership: The person with the most expertise leads via strategic planning and tangible incentives. In short, this leadership style is based on expertise and winning.

Humanistic Leadership: Leadership is not vested in any one person; rather, it emerges from the inclusive collective via consensus in the service of the greater good. In short, this leadership style is based on equality and consensus.

Now that you have a basic idea of what these four styles are, I will elaborate on the simple definitions and add a more detailed description of each style.

Autocratic Leadership

Simple definition: The person with the most power leads via command and control.

Approach: This style reflects a "Unilateral" approach to leadership. When using this style, leaders impose their will through reputation, fear and respect, tightly control information and choices, reward compliance and punish disloyalty. The oldest of the styles, is the way you would expect a ruler (such as a king or dictator) to "rule" their subjects. It is still extremely popular today (both with some rules and also with a surprisingly large percentages of followers and also voters).

Appreciated by: People with predominantly Imperial worldviews who respect dominance and aggression, and who prefer to follow leaders who are perceived as being the strongest, toughest, and most dominant who will be able to protect them from (or defeat) their enemies. Another word for leaders who use this style is "strongman" leaders.

Authoritarian Leadership

This is also known as "Bureaucratic Leadership" and is the term I will often use in this book. It is also known as "authoritative" leadership and "chain of command" leadership.

Simple definition: The person with positional authority leads via chain of command.

Approach: This style reflects a "Hierarchical" approach to leadership. When using this style, leaders compel followers to dutifully comply with the established protocols, coordinate efforts and meet requirements prescribed by authority. This style is the most "parental" of all the styles; the leader is in a position of "parent" and followers are in the position of "child."

Appreciated by: People with Traditional worldviews who value honor, service, loyalty, and conformity, and share traditional beliefs and a willingness to sacrifice now for future rewards... and who prefer to follow leaders who are perceived as having positional and/or moral authority.

Strategic Leadership

This is also known as "Expert Leadership." Some academics who are strongly biased toward the next style (Humanistic) will refer to this style as "Transactional leadership."

Simple definition: The person with the most expertise leads via strategic planning and tangible incentives.

Approach: This style reflects a "Transactional" approach to leadership. When using this style, leaders leverage financial incentives to motivate teams to execute strategic plans in order to outperform competitors.

Appreciated by: People with a Modern worldview who seek opportunities to advance toward their individual goals and who prefer to follow leaders who are perceived as having the most expertise and ability to achieve goals.

Humanistic Leadership

This is also known as "Transformational Leadership," "Collaborative leadership," and "Self-Managed Teams" (the members lead themselves).

Simple definition: Leadership is not vested in any one person; rather, it emerges from the inclusive collective via consensus in the service of the greater good.

Approach: This style reflects a "Transformational" approach to leadership. When using this style, leaders strive for equality and inclusiveness by inviting people's feelings and intuition via dialog to arrive at consensus. This style attempts to draw out the "human potential" of their followers, and work together collaboratively toward common goals. This approach strongly favors "self-managed teams" over "single-leader led teams."

Appreciated by: People with a Postmodern worldview who value diversity, equality, inclusion, authenticity, connection, opportunity for personal growth and contribution to the collective, and who prefer to follow leaders who are perceived as being aware, sensitive to the well-being of others, who strive for consensus, and who always treats others as equals.

Pairing Leadership Styles with Follower Worldviews

Followers with an *Imperial* worldview will find Autocratic leadership credible. These followers look for a leader who is perceived to be powerful and who can protect them from and/or defeat their enemies. If you use any of the other three styles with a person with an Imperial worldview, you run the risk of undermining your credibility with these types of followers.

People with a *Traditional* worldview will find Bureaucratic leadership credible. These followers are looking for a leader who is perceived to have "moral" or positional authority (and the "morals" in this case will always be defined by traditional values and/or traditional religious beliefs. Again, if you use any of the other three styles with a person with a Traditional worldview, you run the risk of undermining your credibility because they won't see you as a legitimate leader (according to what they look for in a leader).

People with a *Modern* worldview will find Strategic leadership credible. These followers are looking for the leader to be the person with the most expertise who is most likely able to help them achieve their goals. Again, if you use any of the other three styles with a person with a Modern worldview, you run the risk of undermining your credibility as you don't exhibit the qualities (and the approaches) that they associate with credible leaders and competent leadership.

People with a *Postmodern* worldview will find Humanistic leadership credible. These followers are looking for the leader to treat everyone as an equal and who strives for equality and consensus. Again, if you use any of the other three styles with a person with a Postmodern worldview, you run the risk of undermining your credibility, as they may not see you as a legitimate leader (they might use the phrase "conscious leader").

The Theorists Are Also Subject to Their Worldviews

By now you are starting to recognize the pattern. The four universal worldviews track perfectly with the four widely acknowledged "paradigms of leadership" put forth by the different experts. As I will explain in this book, the theorists who put forth leadership theories are often subject to their own worldview biases. The advocates of the different approaches (or styles of leadership) can be seen clearly to hold these different worldviews. In most cases their bias is unconscious and they do not admit or acknowledge the existence of the other three worldviews. And they certainly don't agree that the other leadership paradigms (other than the one they are biased towards) hold any merit at all. This is of course ridiculous and reflects the fact that they are leaving out the context dimension of leadership.

Perhaps most embarrassing of all, many so-called leadership experts and leadership training programs seem to leave out followers altogether! Even many of the most respected leadership authorities have overlooked this pattern that the follower's mindset (worldview) determines, in large part, which "leadership paradigm" will offer the most utility in that context.

This chapter has introduced you to Integral Leadership. This is an important topic that warrants a much longer treatment. If this interests you, see my book, *Integral Leadership: The World's First Unifying Theory of Leadership That Will Forever Transform How You Understand, Practice and Develop Leadership*

We are now ready to assemble the "Universal Leadership Model!" As a way to help you not only fully understand the model but also to appreciate the relationships between its different components, I will walk you through a logical, step-by-step process of building the model section-by-section in the next chapter.

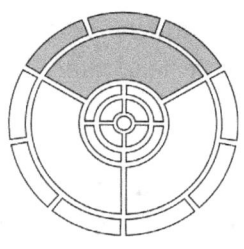

CHAPTER 3:
THE UNIVERSAL LEADERSHIP MODEL

When we combine the "Leadership Rosetta Stone", which clearly articulates four distinct approaches to leadership, with the three "Inherent Leadership Responsibilities" and the nine "Essential Leadership Skills", you have what I call the "Universal Leadership Model." All leaders everywhere, regardless of context, share these three inherent leadership responsibilities. All leaders fulfill their responsibilities by engaging in the activities we see under each of the nine leadership skill sets (also called "core competencies").

Naturally, the activities, techniques and skills may use different names, but the work of leadership is universal, and the skills leaders need to be effective are also universal.

What is different from culture to culture and leader to leader is the "approach" or the "style" with which they undertake these activities.

A leader can engage the activities associated with each skill set using any of the four universal leadership styles: *Autocratic,*

Bureaucratic, Strategic, and *Humanistic,* which track perfectly with the four predominant leadership paradigms we explored previously.

While this may sound quite straightforward, my colleagues and I are the only ones who are approaching leadership and leadership development in this uniquely effective way.

Our *Universal Leadership Model* is an "integrally-informed" approach to leadership. In the year 2000, I created a one-year training program called "The Integral Leadership Program" and launched a leadership academy with my close friend Rand Stagen to bring this approach to the business world with the goal of helping to "make business a force for good." As of this writing, more than two thousand companies (and growing) have adopted this approach.

This "integral" or "conscious" approach to leadership played a central role in helping to launch and grow the "Conscious Capitalism" movement (also known as the "Conscious Business Movement). I mention this to highlight the fact that this is not merely a model or framework. This approach to leadership and leadership development that is not "theoretical;" rather, it is tried and proven to be extraordinarily effective over more than two decades with thousands of companies including non-profit companies and other types of organizations around the world, even in developing countries. Many people familiar with the field of leadership development believe that this approach is one of the most effective, if not <u>the</u> most effective approach to leadership development that exists.

In this chapter we will assemble the "Universal Leadership Model" from the components we have already introduced: 1) The Leadership Rosetta Stone, 2) Inherent Leadership Responsibilities and 3) Leadership Core Competencies. For clarity's sake, I will bring one element in at a time, illustrate each, and then combine them as we assemble the model.

First, recall the four universal leadership styles: *Strategic, Humanistic, Bureaucratic* and *Autocratic.*

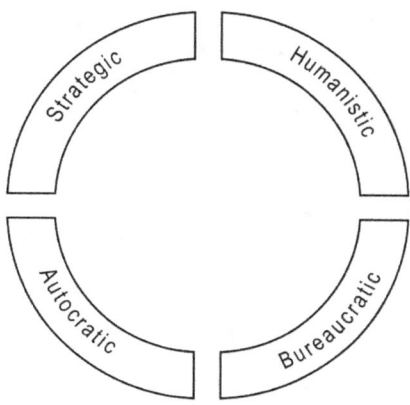

Next, the *Leadership Rosetta Stone* revealed the four predominant "follower worldviews." And we learned that each worldview has a specific definition of legitimate leadership and is looking for very different things in people who they view as credible leaders.

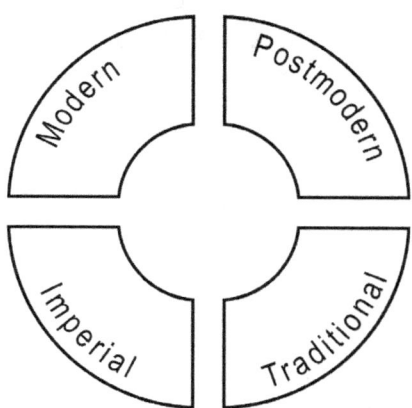

We now recognize that for leadership to be viewed as effective (by those being led), the correct leadership style must be paired with the follower's worldview (which dictates how they define effective leadership and what they look for in a credible leader. When we bring the styles and the worldviews together, we can illustrate it like this.

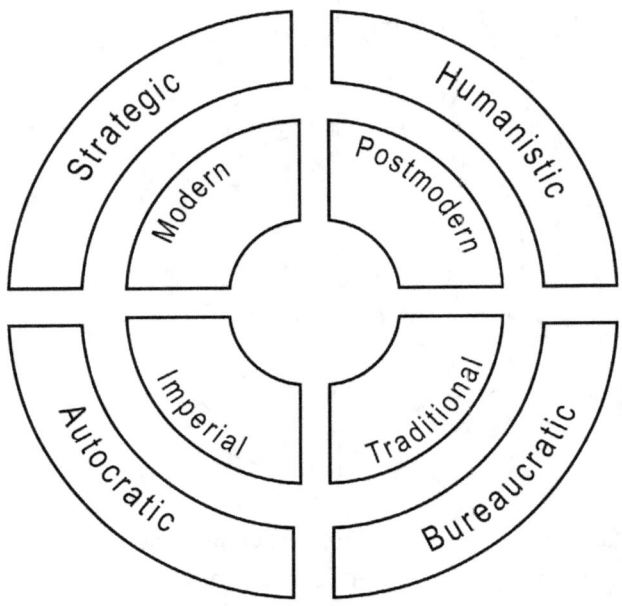

In the above illustration we can see that the correct leadership style is paired with the worldview of the follower (according to the style of leadership that follower will view as credible and legitimate).

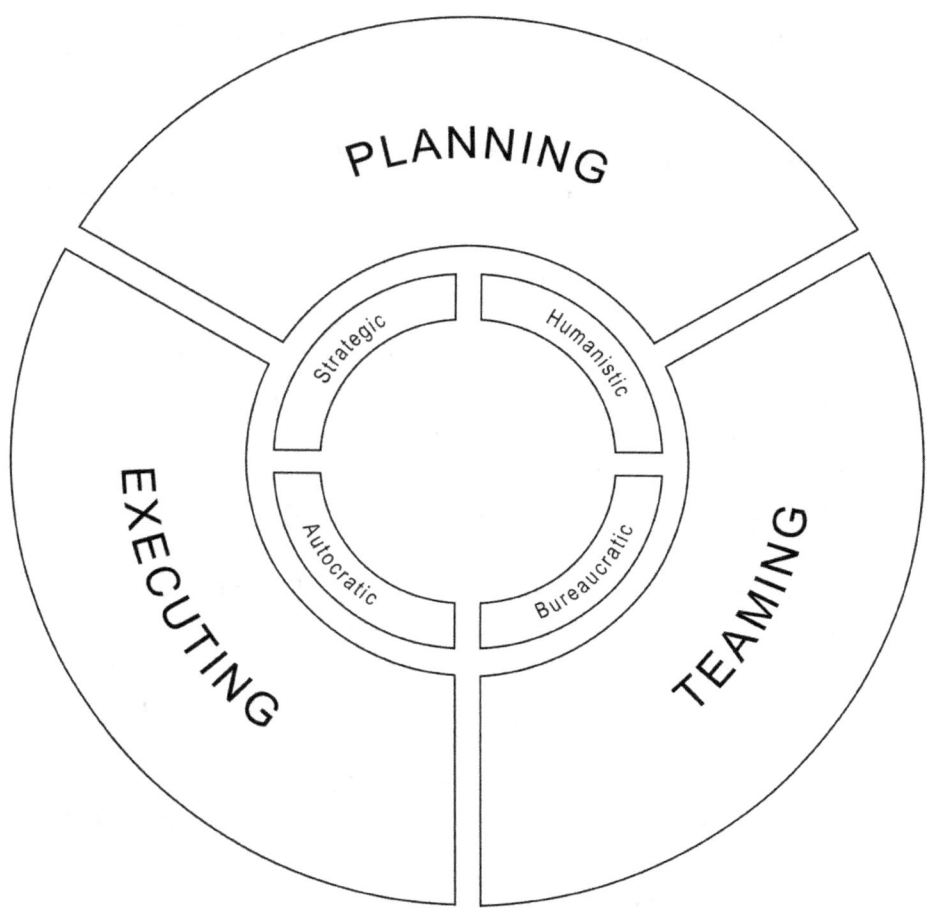

Next, you will recall that there are three "Inherent Leadership Responsibilities," which point to the three "Essential Abilities" all leaders must possess to be considered competent and adequately well-rounded leaders.

Using common terms, those are often referred to as *Planning, Teaming* and *Executing*. I introduce additional, more nuanced terms in Chapter 4: Accelerating Leadership.

When you take into account the leadership style, you can see that different types of leaders will take a different approach, that is, use a different style as they fulfill these responsibilities. Put another way, all leaders demonstrate three essential abilities, but they use different styles.

For example, one leader may use a "Humanistic" approach to *planning, teaming* and *executing*. Another leader may use an "Autocratic" approach, another a "Strategic" approach and another a "Bureaucratic" approach.

This fact is reflected in our illustration with the four different styles pictured inside the three responsibilities. While this is a static illustration, you might want to imagine the center circle (with the leadership styles) spinning around so that different styles can be deployed with different areas of responsibilities.

Sadly, some leaders lack any versatility at all, and always use their native style (example: Strategic) with all followers. The result of only using one style is that it is only resonant with those followers who have that corresponding worldview (values and beliefs). For the other estimated 25-75% of the people in typical diverse organizations (who have a different worldview), that leader's style comes across as ineffective, out of touch, lame, not trustworthy, clueless or even foolish. Imagine how ridiculous the positional, "parental," authoritarian style comes across to postmodern followers who despise hierarchy and believe that legitimate leaders always treat everyone as equals. Get it?

Versatile leaders (this includes all leaders who have had the benefit of my Integral Leadership training) develop much-needed capacity to switch their style up and emphasize different leadership styles with different people and circumstances, as the situation warrants. For example, they can adopt a more Strategic style with their modern worldview, goal-oriented, success-driven followers, and then they lean on a more Humanistic style with their postmodern worldview, progressive followers who expect to be treated as an equal (and expect their feelings and perspectives to be respected and taken into account on all major organizational decisions). And that same versatile leader will adopt a more "hierarchical" Bureaucratic approach with their Traditional worldview followers who see legitimate leaders as using their positional authority to enforce rules and compliance.

Next, you will recall that for each of the inherent leadership responsibilities, that leaders engage a variety of practices, activities, skill sets and/or "competencies" to fulfill their responsibilities. In our pragmatic framework, we describe three skill sets for each of the three responsibilities (3 skill sets x 3 responsibilities = 9 total skill sets).

Each of these nine skill sets consist of about half a dozen techniques (behaviors, not concepts). I go into much more detail about these techniques in my other books. This book focuses on the "Strategy & Alignment" dimension.

This next simplified illustration shows the three essential abilities (in the middle area) along with the nine skill sets around the outer ring).

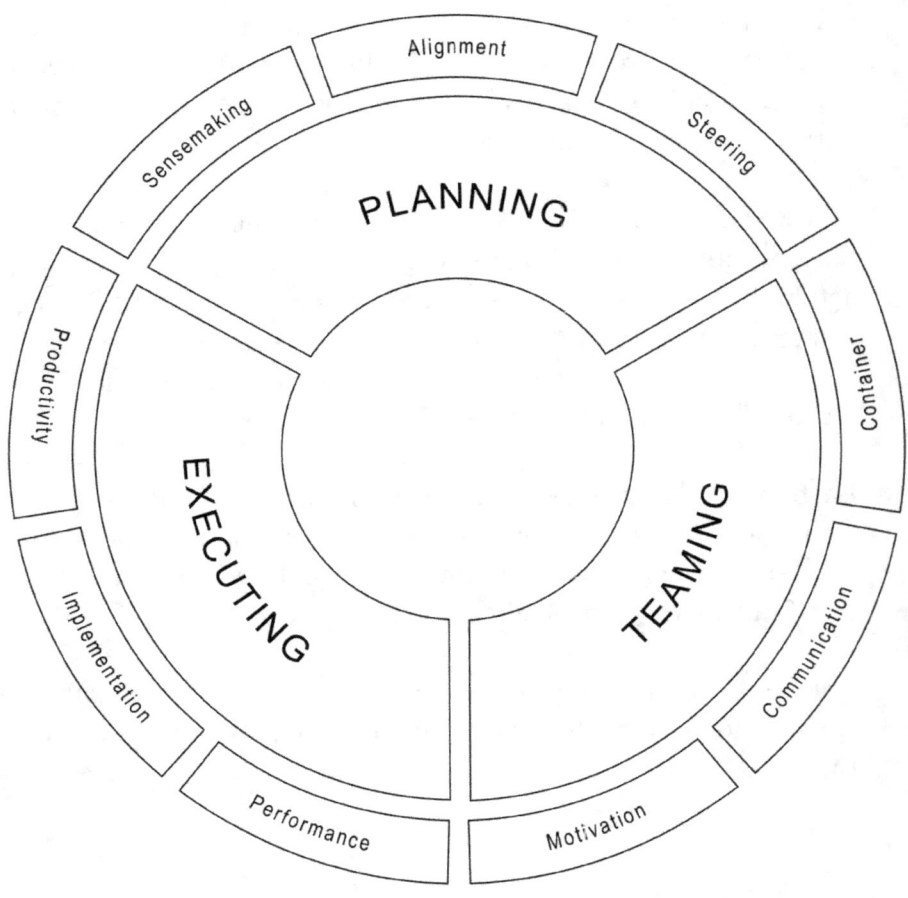

Next, we will want to bring the four leadership styles and four follower worldviews back into our illustration. This way, our illustration reflects that leaders can engage their three "essential abilities" (*planning, teaming* and *executing*) in the middle of the diagram, along with their corresponding (3x3) skill sets along the outer ring using any of these leadership styles, and those styles should be paired up correctly based on the followers being led.

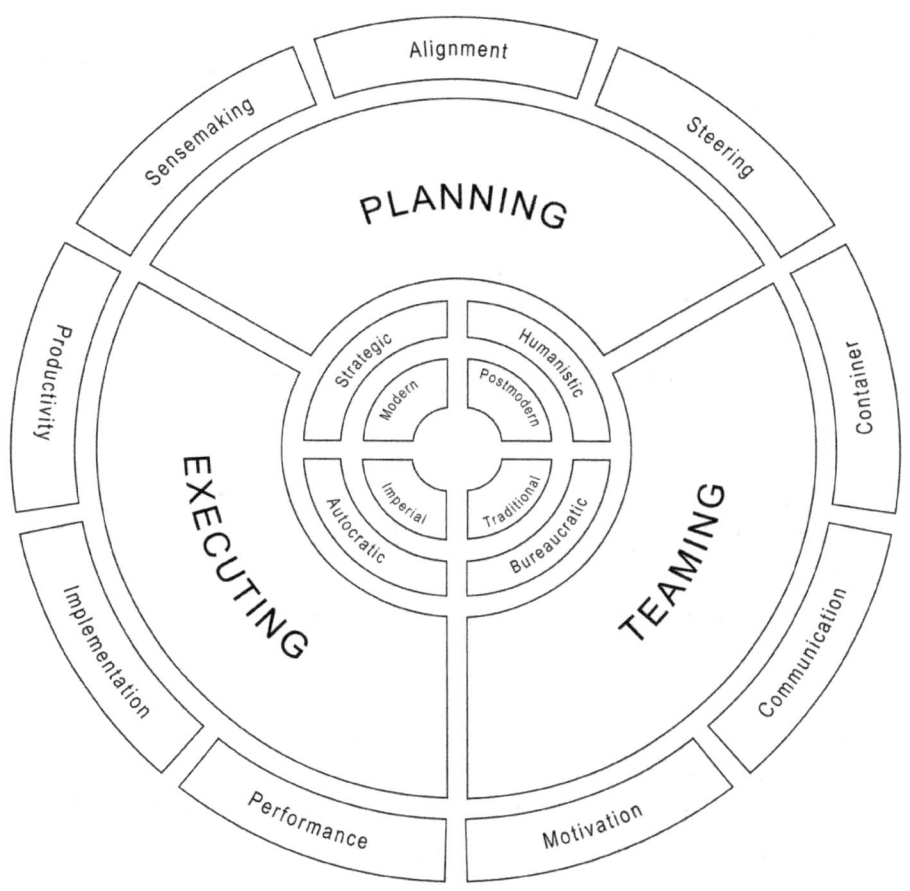

Like so. Now, this version of the model visually suggests that for each ability (middle section) and for each of the nine skill sets (outer section), there are four different styles to draw upon.

For example, there is a "Authority" way to hold people accountable for job performance and a "strategic" way to hold people accountable for their performance. There is an "autocratic" approach to creating the team "container" and there is a "humanistic" approach to creating a container (and they are as different as night and day). Similarly, there is a "humanistic" way to approach alignment around vision, for example, and there is a "strategic" way to approach coming up with the vision and aligning people around it. As a final example, there is an autocratic way to motivate people and teams, a bureaucratic way, and of course a more humanistic way.

Once you have experience working with this framework, you will realize it provides a nearly unlimited amount of versatility to the art and science of leadership. Mastering this approach will enable you to be an effective leader with a diverse population of followers. Eventually you will be able to influence, motivate, inspire and guide just about anyone, regardless of their worldview.

At first, this notion of leading with the requisite versatility of shifting from "Strategic" style to the "Humanistic" or "Bureaucratic" style appears difficult. Yet, my 22 years of teaching leaders to do this shows that it is actually easier than it looks. It just takes instruction from someone who knows this framework, and a lot of practice.

Simply put, to expand your versatility, you will need to select the next style you want to master, find a role model to emulate (and/or read my other books or take one of my many courses), and then practice the new style until it feels natural.

Here is a slightly longer instruction on how to do this.

Recall that the three most common worldviews in most organizations are *Traditional, Modern* and *Postmodern*. The good news is you already have one style down, I call that one your "native style." It is likely either Strategic or Humanistic (that pairs with the Modern and Postmodern follower worldviews respectively). If your role models were highly traditional, then maybe your native style is Bureaucratic (also called Authoritarian). That hierarchical style must only be used with followers with Traditional worldviews. (The other types of followers will find that "parental" approach quite off-putting, especially the postmodern types who hate hierarchy and expect legitimate leaders to treat everyone as an equal.)

Now, after you identify your "native" style, reflect on your team, organization and the followers you interact with the most.

In this example, I will assume your native style is Strategic. Well, you certainly have all the followers in your organization who have a Modern worldview covered.

What's the next largest group?

Is it Postmodern? If you work in tech or with a younger workforce (millennials and Gen Z) then you probably work with a lot of followers with the postmodern worldview. So then the "Humanistic" style is the one you want to master next!

The best way to learn that style (besides taking one of my courses) is to identify other leaders in your organization, and teachers and mentors, who are "fluent in that values dialect" and who either use the Humanistic style natively or have mastered it through practice.

Study them, notice how they always say "we" and almost never say "I". Notice how they let everyone else speak <u>first</u> before they speak. (Autocratic and Authoritarian leaders would never do that.) Pay attention to how these "Humanistic" leaders demonstrate respect for everyone's perspective, how they treat everyone as their equal, and how they strive for consensus.

Also notice the way that they hold people accountable, delegate, give feedback, motivate, handle group decisions and just about every other leader responsibility and activity is undertaken in a slightly different way than you do (contrasting the Humanistic style with the Strategic style in this hypothetical example).

The details of their Humanistic style should be obvious now that I have given you the "leadership styles cheat codes" in the form of my Leadership Rosetta Stone). The answers are all around you, you just needed to know what to look for. And now you know exactly what to look for.

Before we move on, there are still two more elements to represent in the "Universal Leadership Model" that we have started to assemble.

Can you guess what is still missing in our illustration so far?

We have covered *followers, leadership styles, leadership responsibilities* and *leadership skills.* Recall the element that our leadership industry whistleblowers from Harvard and Stanford (Keller and Pfeffer) point out that is often ignored. Perhaps you guessed it. Recall what Lewin ignored when he studied young children doing arts and crafts to create a model of corporate leadership styles.

Did you guess it?

It is "organizational context" (or what I also call "circumstances").

Whether or not a given leader and their style (or approach) will be effective is largely a function of the context (the circumstances). As history has shown us repeatedly, an incompetent, failed, and discredited leader in one context will be heralded as a brilliant successful leader in a different context (with a different audience). Or the opposite, a leader may be very successful in one context and a dismal failure in another.

So when we add organizational context (circumstances) to our Universal Leadership Model it looks like this.

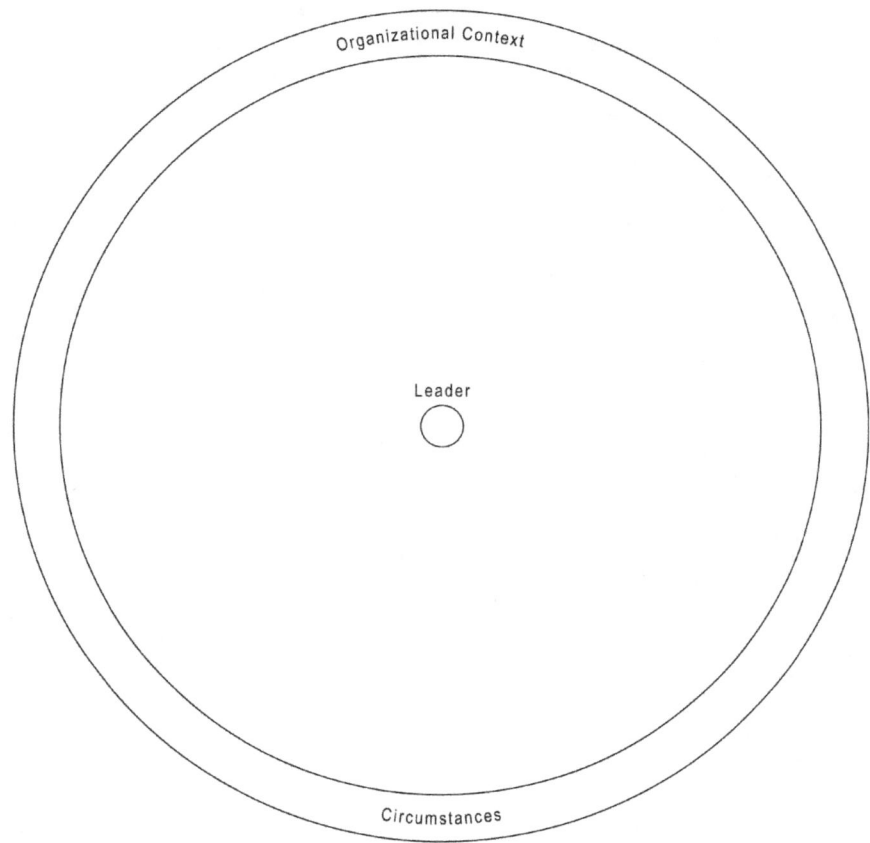

There is just one last element to add to our illustration. This last element, the leader, bears special emphasis. In this illustration you can see the leader (represented by small circle in the middle).

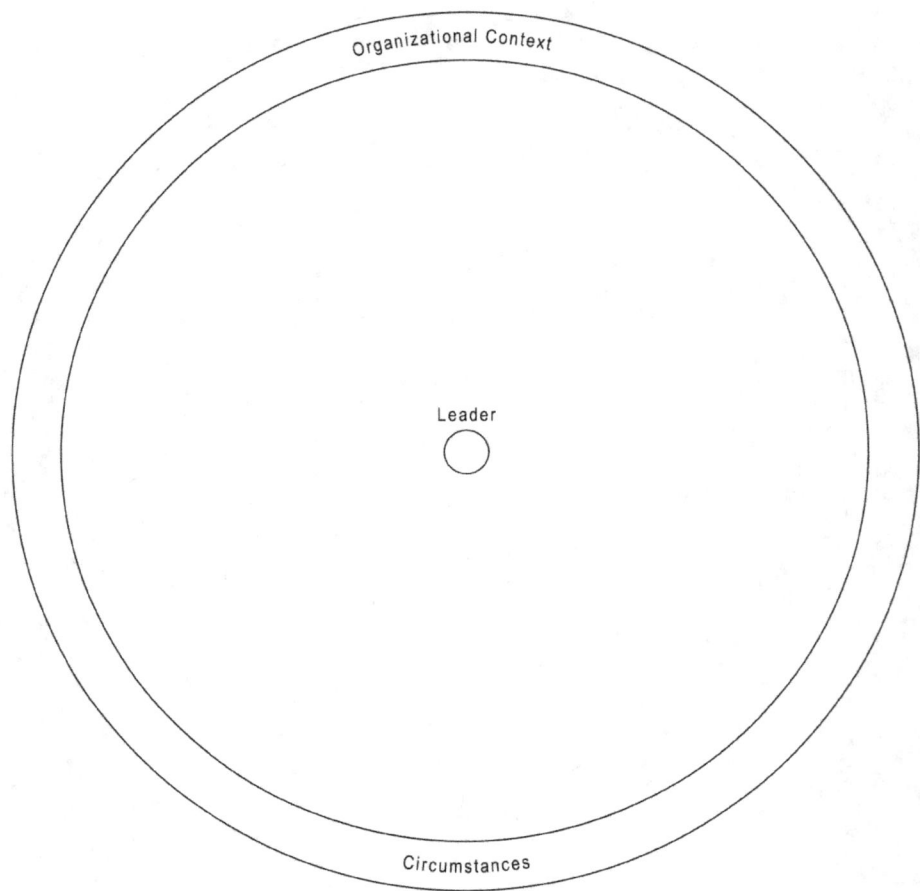

To be effective, this leader must first and foremost be able to make sense out of their circumstances. In many of our courses and coaching programs, we go into much detail about sensemaking. (You may recall it is one of the nine core competencies). Sensemaking is the leadership skill that leaders must draw upon to make sense of the context (their circumstances). In our leadership courses and coaching programs, we encourage leaders to ask the following questions:

What is really happening?
What is important?
What is needed?

And...
What is the most helpful action I can take?

The next important thing for a leader to understand after understanding the organizational context, is...

Who are the followers that they wish to influence (or lead)?

The most important thing about a follower's psychological makeup is their worldview because it determines which of the four universal leadership styles they will strongly prefer (and willingly follow). The next logical piece of the Universal Leadership Model to bring in will be the followers.

The next logical piece of the Universal Leadership Model to bring in will be the <u>followers</u>."

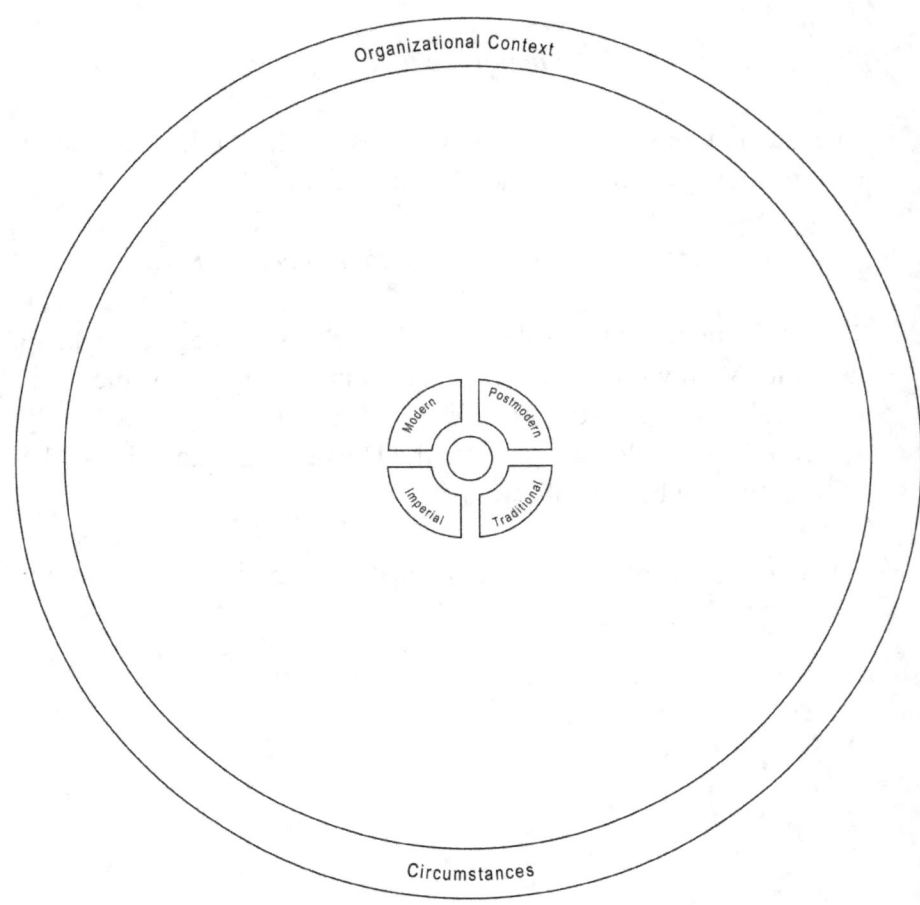

Leaders who are viewed as "credible" by followers when the leaders use the leadership style preferred by those followers (indicated in the diagram by the appropriate leadership styles being paired with follower worldviews.)

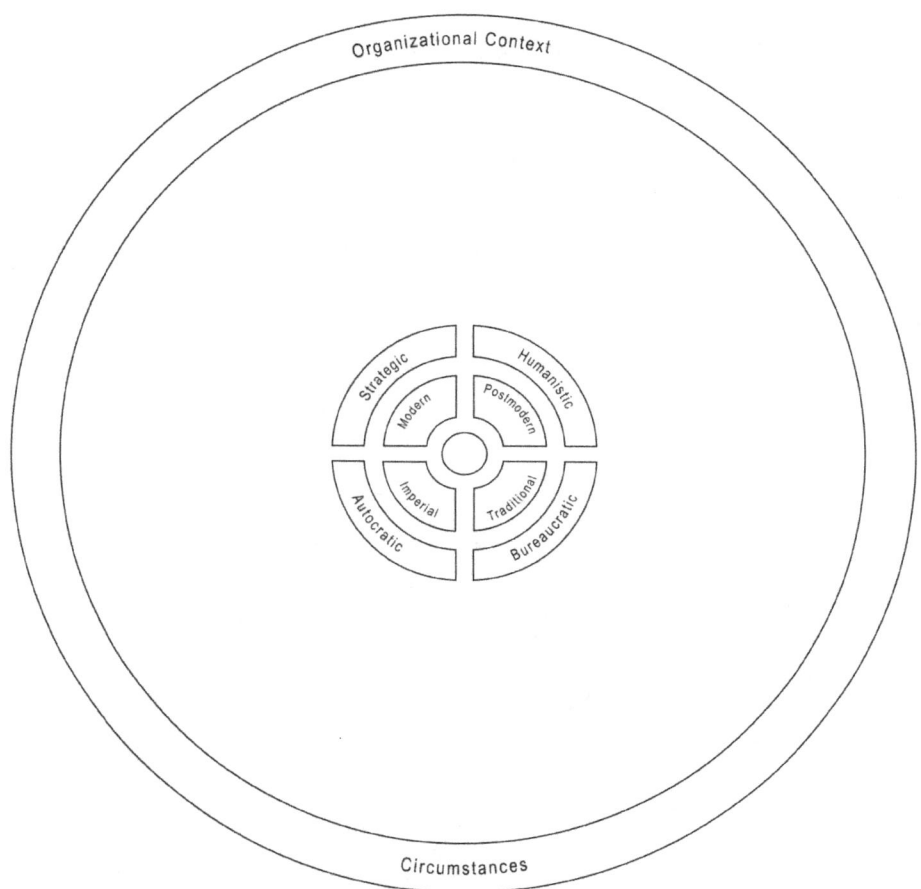

At this point, you should already know what comes next in our model. Leaders have three "inherent leadership responsibilities," also called three "essential abilities" they draw upon to fulfill their responsibilities.

The way they approach those responsibilities is a function of their "leadership style."

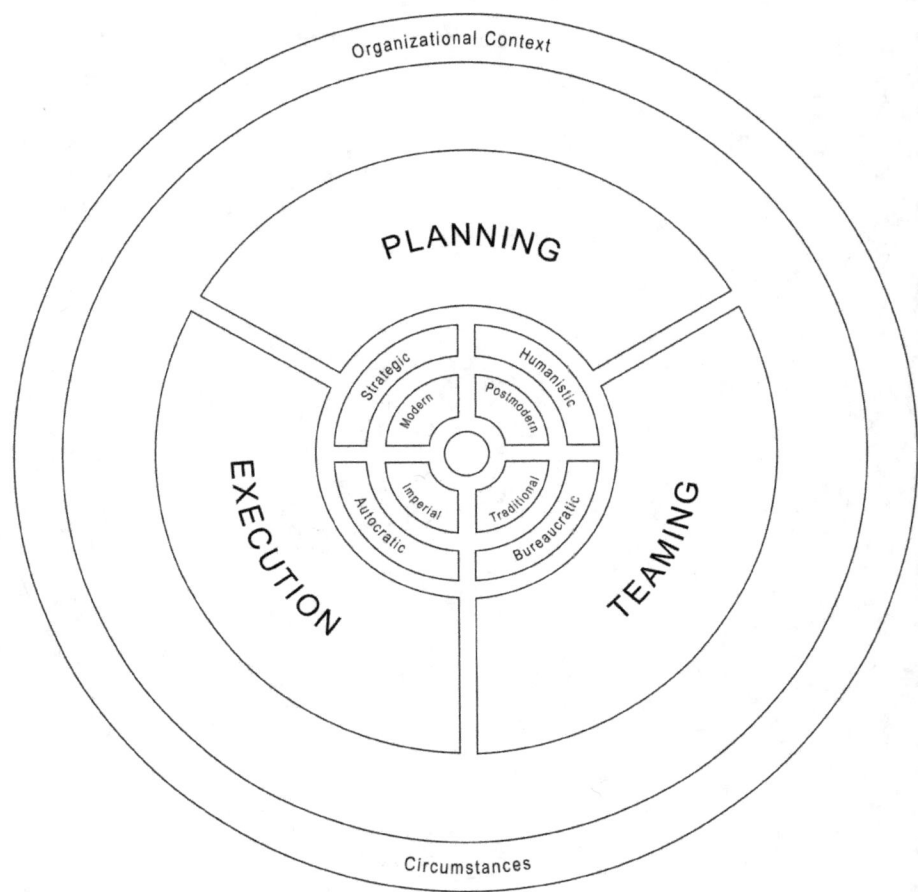

The words Planning, Teaming and Execution represent the "inherent leadership responsibilities" and also the "essential leader abilities."

Next, we know that leaders must engage in many activities, and use their "skill sets" in order to fulfill those responsibilities. Of course, each of these skill sets looks different according to the leadership style being used.

Once we bring these nine skill sets back in, we have the full Universal Leadership Model.

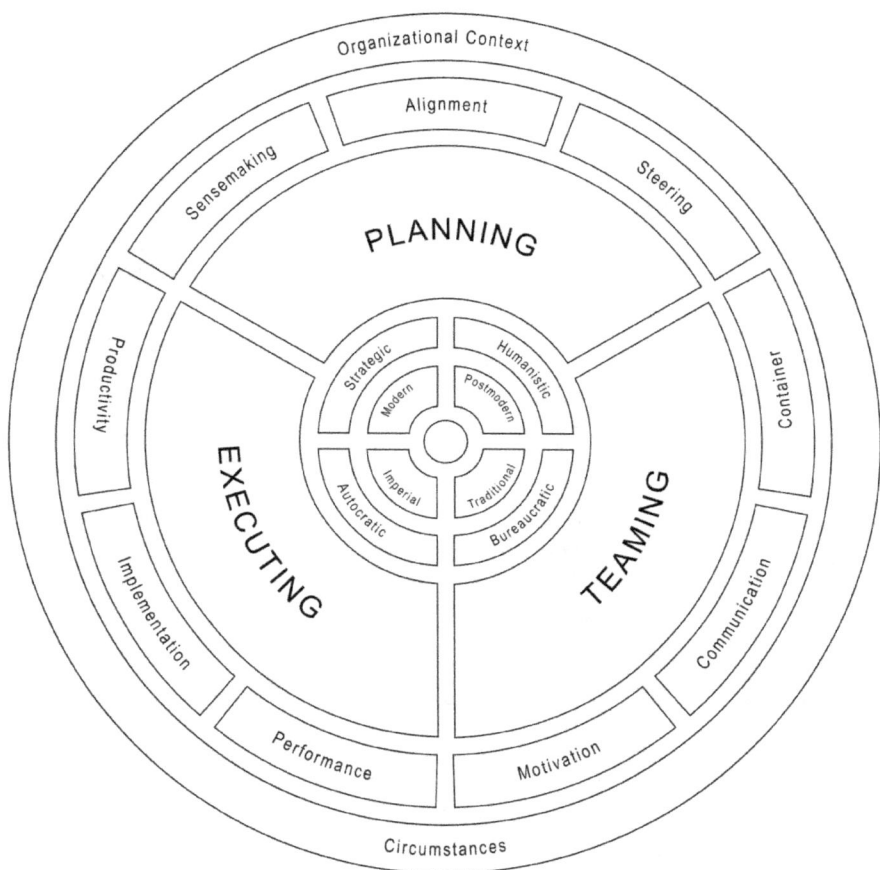

Please study this simple, yet profound, model. If you learn and apply it, it will revolutionize your leadership. This chapter provides a high-level overview of the Universal Leadership Model.

This model merits a longer discussion. If you would like to continue this discussion, with more detail and nuance, please refer to my other book, *The Universal Leadership Model: The Simplicity on the Other Side of Complexity*.

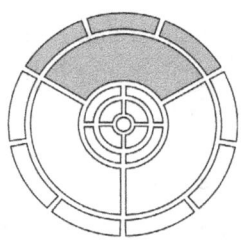

CHAPTER 4:
THE INTEGRAL LEADERSHIP METHODOLOGY

Previously, I introduced the three inherent leadership responsibilities. In this chapter, I will expand upon them to unpack the most common skill sets that leaders draw upon to fulfill those responsibilities, and I will introduce the world's fastest and most effective method for improving leadership performance and organizational results. In this chapter, you will be introduced to the "practice-based leadership" approach that I invented in the early 2000s at Stagen Leadership Academy and Integral Institute. As you are about to see in this chapter, this is an absolute game-changer.

As mentioned in an earlier, "character traits" or vague "leadership qualities" can't be taught or learned in any reasonable amount of time. But "technique" (also known as behavior, or practices) can absolutely be trained and learned relatively quickly. This is the key to rapid leadership development.

I'm going to be blunt again here.

Please stop listening to bogus leadership advice from the leadership industry's "snake oil salesmen" who push vague concepts like EQ, confidence, trustworthiness, or charisma.

Vague concepts have never helped a leader increase this technical and complex skill. Seek advice from people who have legitimate expertise in the requisite leadership skills and "techniques" and know how to help clients develop those skills (by teaching the requisite techniques, not vague concepts).

"What, abandon EQ" you might be saying to yourself? No, of course you don't abandon your ability for emotional intelligence.

Of course, emotional intelligence is important... that is the <u>capacity</u> that we point to when we use the term emotional intelligence is important... along with *social intelligence, cognitive intelligence, moral intelligence,* and so on.

I realize these intelligences are important. In fact, I have taught and written extensively about these human capacities over the last two decades. My colleagues and I have developed assessments to measure low, medium and high levels of development along these intelligences (which integral and developmental psychologists call "lines of development").

However, and this is the key point, in my 20+ years I've <u>never</u> ever, not even once, seen a person's EQ improve by lecturing them about what it is.

Stop talking about emotional intelligence. You are wasting your breath and the listener's time, attention and energy.

This is a somewhat nuanced but extremely important point I am making here.

This lies at the heart of what is wrong with the leadership development industry.

> *Talking about intelligence does nothing to increase it. This is akin to taking piano lessons and the instructor talks about the qualities of great piano players. The instructor goes on and on of the benefit of "musical intelligence."*

It is so obvious when we talk about other technical and complex skills (playing a musical instrument, learning to play a sport like baseball or basketball, or learning karate).

But when we talk about the technical and complex skill of leadership, people somehow miss the obvious fact that we are talking about a technical and complex skill made up of techniques and skills.

> *If you went to basketball camp, the instructors would not talk about "athletic intelligence" (kinesthetic intelligence). Rather, you would practice dribbling, passing, shooting and rebounding!*

The only time you should be talking about intelligences or "leadership traits" is when you are creating a profile for hiring. If you are in a hiring role, then yes, you want to screen and hire people with high EQ.

This book is about leadership development.

Emotional intelligence improves when and only when you give a person a specific technique, a practice, to adopt and use daily over many months.

This is the only way to improve these skills: through practice.

Most leadership training and coaching programs talk about "EQ" (and trust and culture and inclusivity and so on) as vague concepts and very few offer specific techniques as daily practices that actually grow these capacities.

This is the key distinction you must grasp to appreciate this groundbreaking leadership development approach.

If your objective is to improve your leadership skills rapidly, then you will want to put most of the emphasis on the specific skill sets you need to enhance the abilities you are targeting. We must come down out of the clouds of vague concepts into specific behaviors that can be memorized, practiced and matured with time (and with which we can layer on additional skills that comprise the complex abilities we associate with leadership). I previously introduced three responsibilities that have always been and always will be inherent to leadership. I call these the three *Inherent Responsibilities of Leadership*.

While these three inherent responsibilities go by many names, I have been using the common terms of *planning, teaming* and *executing*.

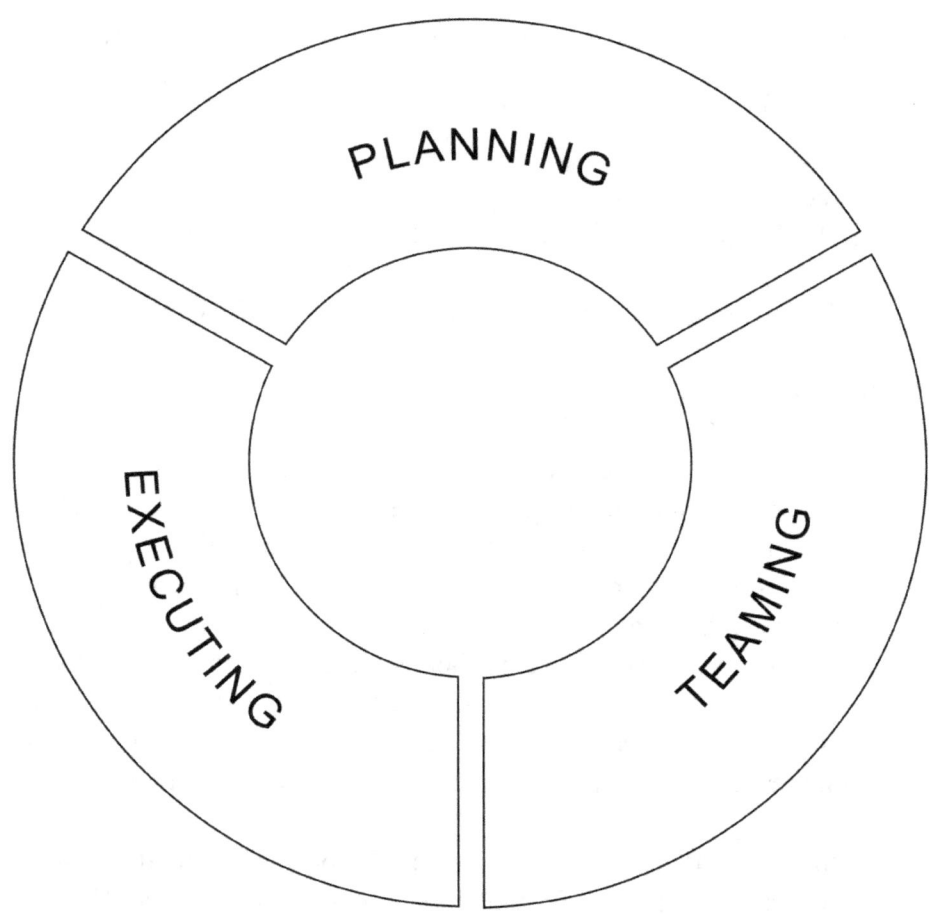

I will now begin the pivot from conventional, common ways of describing these "activities" to our more nuanced names and descriptions.

1. Planning

You will recall that leaders articulate a vision (a direction) and suggest some kind of plan to achieve that vision. They also have to align stakeholders with values and purpose of the organization and cultivate their commitment to that vision or direction, and they must guide or "steer" the organization toward that vision over time. For simplicity's sake and to feel familiar to the widest population of book readers, I've gone with the single word "planning" here, but the word "steering" would be another one-word way to describe this responsibility.

A more comprehensive and accurate title for this first dimension of leadership responsibility would be *"Strategy & Alignment."*

This is the main focus of this book you are currently reading.

2. Teaming

You will recall that leaders "create the container" and "set the tone" of the relationships among the team members. The leader establishes some kind of structure for the team(s) including the norms that people are expected to follow in terms of supporting, relating, communicating and motivating. This may be explicitly communicated or simply be implicit (setting the example that others can follow). Think of this group of activities as the interpersonal dimension of leadership. I've used the word "teaming" here, but some readers may be more resonant with the word "relating."

A more comprehensive and accurate title for this second dimension of leadership responsibility would be *"Teamwork & Culture."*

This is the subject of my book entitled: *Teamwork & Culture: How the Most Successful Leaders Set People Up for Success, Cultivate High Performance Teamwork and Leverage Communication Versatility to Keep Everyone Engaged and Motivated.*

3. Executing

As we saw earlier, this area of leadership responsibility includes guiding productive work to execute the strategy (implement the plans), managing people's performance and the projects they are working on. It is concerned with all of the activities an organization engages in, that have to do managing projects using the appropriate tools to coordinate work across teams, meeting expectations and being able to hold each other accountable to tasks, milestones, and deadlines, and making sure that people are focused on the right things and staying productive, efficient and effective. Some people think of this as "operational leadership". You may have heard the term "boots on the ground." You might also think of this dimension as the "hands" and "feet" of leadership.

A more comprehensive and accurate title for this third dimension of leadership responsibility would be *"Execution & Performance."*

This is the subject of my other book entitled: *Execution & Performance: How the Most Successful Leaders Close Employee Performance Gaps, Maintain Accountability and High Productivity, and Consistently Deliver Exceptional Results.*

In the next section, I will pass across these three again, this time making them more comprehensive and accurate, as leadership literature would describe them, and offer a more detailed description of many of the "activities" that leaders engage in order to fulfill these responsibilities. This convention of "activities" will become extremely important.

As mentioned before, stories of great leaders and descriptions of leaders' personality traits do little (if anything) to help you become a better leader. But if you understand the activities that effective leaders do, and you learn the specific techniques (behaviors) they leverage to complete those activities successfully, then you can rapidly improve your leadership ability.

Clearly there are a lot of leadership activities that fall into these three groupings. These three abilities are comprised of skill sets, and the skill sets are, in turn, comprised of about half a dozen discrete skills (methods or techniques that have been internalized to the point that they are instinctual).

If you survey the literature on leadership, you would find dozens of discrete techniques, tactics or skills related to each of these three fundamental categories.

While there is an infinite number of techniques, methods and skills for each of these skill sets, we have found, applying Pareto's law, that it boils down to only about half a dozen specific leadership techniques / skills that matter most (for each of the nine skill sets).

This process is related to "Complex Skill Instructional Design" we discussed in the introduction chapter. This is how we learn to play baseball (throwing, catching, batting, running) or to play a musical instrument (playing notes, combining notes into chords, musical theory of keys and chord progressions, and combining these elements into songs).

> *To repeat, it is impossible to learn a complex skill (sports, martial arts, playing an instrument, flying an airplane or leadership) without breaking the complex skill down into its component parts, and then learning the technique that support each of those skills.*

Think of it this way. You and every leader you have ever worked with (or for) has drawn on these skill sets (by whatever name) to fulfill their leadership responsibilities. You may be wondering about level of skill, or level of competency. You are right to recognize that natural talent in each of these skill set areas is not evenly distributed across the population.

While all leaders engage in some version of these activities which are inherent to leadership, some are very skillful and others have not had the benefit of training and mentorship, and who may not have strong natural instincts in that area.

For example, every leader "motivates" their followers in one way or another without exception.

Similarly, even if a leader does not have any natural ability or formal training in "planning," they still make plans in some way, even if those plans are very rudimentary. Even an unsophisticated leader would say, "This is my plan."

A final example is communication. Without exception, all leaders draw upon whatever communication skills they have to coordinate efforts.

It bears repeating that these three inherent leadership responsibilities and nine skill sets are universal. Talent, training and competency level are not universal.

Some of the leaders you worked with (and for) may have been terrible at sensemaking, alignment, strategic thinking, and planning. But if they were in a leadership role for long, they were in fact doing some version of the activities that fall into that 'bucket' we call sensemaking, alignment, strategic thinking, and planning.

In my other books, I define exactly what competency looks like at lower, intermediate, and higher levels of proficiency for each of the three essential abilities and all nine core competencies. While this book on Strategy & Alignment details out the benchmarks in this dimension, if you want to see the benchmarks for the other two dimensions of leadership, you can find them in my other books titled *Teamwork & Culture* and *Execution & Performance* (or see the conclusion section of this book for reference of my other books).

But let's not get ahead of ourselves. For now, it is helpful to just recognize the fact that these nine skill sets are fundamental to leadership and, in turn, organizational life.

You are already doing these nine things. All leaders (who are competent enough to stay in a leadership role for very long) do some versions of these nine activities in order to fulfill their responsibilities.

To provide more nuance, rather than limit ourselves to the common and familiar way of naming and thinking about each of these nine fundamental leadership skill sets, in the next section, we will introduce new terms and descriptions.

Now, continuing with our review of the essential abilities and core competencies, we will expand beyond the familiar or common labels and introduce our own terms.

For example, "Performance" becomes "Performance Management." "Alignment" becomes "Stakeholder Alignment." "Implementation" becomes "Project Implementation." And "planning" becomes "Dynamic Steering."

We are now going through another pass across the three essential abilities which represent the three buckets of activities, and the three skill sets (core competencies of leadership) under each.

We begin with the dimension I have been referring to simply as "Planning."

Strategy & Alignment

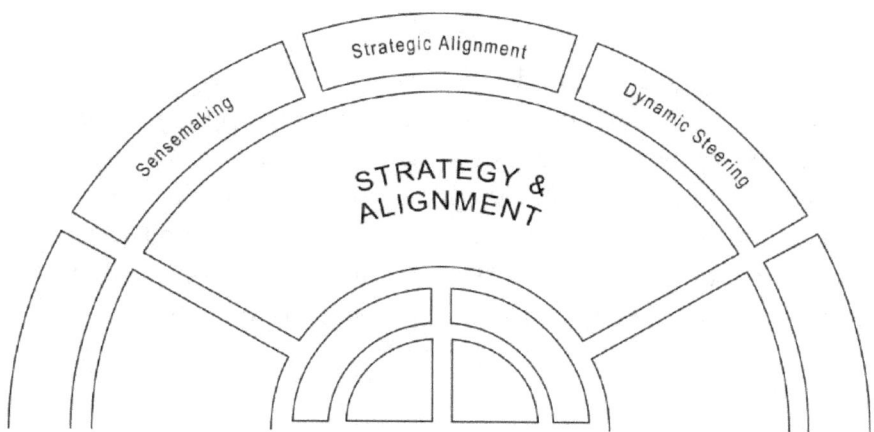

In our first pass, I called this area of responsibility simply "Planning." I will now introduce the more nuanced term, *Strategy & Alignment*.

You will recall that I defined this area of responsibility as: *establishing vision and goals, crafting strategy and plans, and enrolling stakeholder commitment.*

As we will see in this part of the book, *Strategy & Alignment* includes all of the activities related to: establishing and communicating the purpose, vision, and values of the organization, making sense of what is happening in the current environment including evaluating relevant challenges and opportunities, strategic thinking, prioritizing strategic objectives, crafting strategic plans, and enrolling stakeholder commitment in the organizational vision and the strategy to achieve shared goals.

As mentioned previously, because these skill sets are fundamental and universal, you should be able to recognize the activities in each "bucket" because they are activities that you and every other leader does in one way or another (perhaps by a different name). As we unpack each skill set in later chapters, we will weave in leadership best practices which are the behaviors that skillful leaders engage when drawing upon this skill set to fulfill their leadership responsibilities.

As the saying goes, "repetition is the mother of skill." I am sure you are aware of the benefit of revisiting and reviewing key concepts, especially, as we layer in additional distinctions. I will use this convention often in this book by re-introducing previous concepts and adding another layer of nuance. As we make a second pass over these core competencies, I will replace the simple, commonly used terms introduced previously with my more nuanced terms.

Sensemaking

This skill set is concerned with your ability to evaluate the landscape (both external conditions as well as internal organizational dynamics) to determine what is really happening, the key drivers impacting the environment, what is most important for your organization, and what is most needed.

Stakeholder Alignment

This skill set is concerned with your ability to establish and articulate your organization's direction in the form of vision, values and purpose, then to align all key stakeholders so that they feel and demonstrate a shared commitment to it.

Organizational Steering

This skill set is concerned with your ability to develop and evolve organizational strategies, establish and revise goals and objectives, and prioritize the highest-leverage projects that will lead to desired outcomes each quarter and each year.

Teamwork & Culture

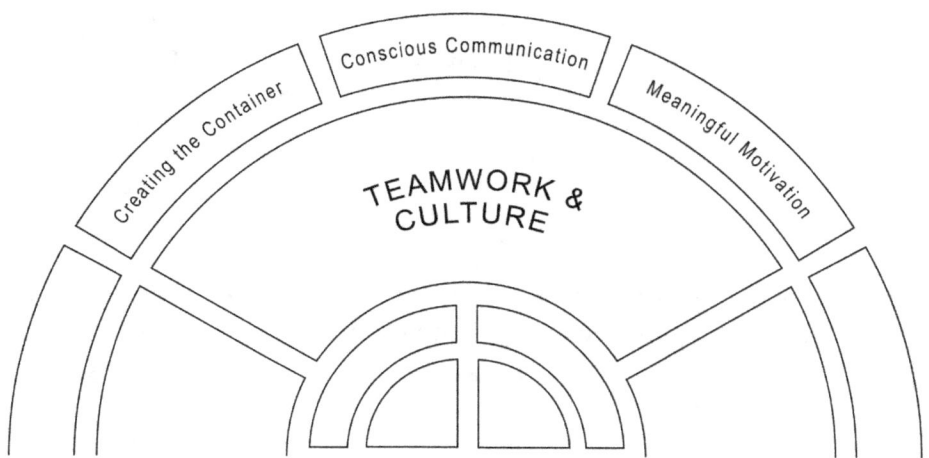

In our first pass, I called this area of responsibility and this "essential ability" simply "Teaming." I will now introduce a more nuanced term, "Teamwork & Culture."

I define this area of responsibility as: *Setting your team(s) up for success with the appropriate structure and culture, and supporting and communicating with them to keep them optimally engaged and motivated.*

Teamwork & Culture includes all of the activities related to setting your people up for success, creating and maintaining a conducive environment including a healthy culture and emotional climate, keeping people engaged and motivated using appropriate and effective communication, including feedback, listening, collaboration, and managing conflict.

Next, I will very briefly introduce each of the three skill sets that leaders draw upon to fulfill their responsibilities associated with this dimension. And I will replace the commonly-used terms, with more nuanced names.

Creating the Container

This skill set is concerned with your ability to set people up for success— this includes equipping teams with the structure, culture, training, tools and support they need to achieve shared organizational goals.

Communication

This skill set is concerned with effective communication which involves social awareness, listening, framing, feedback, dialog, collaboration, working with assumptions and interpretations, and managing conflict.

Motivation

This skill set is concerned with keeping people engaged and motivated by understanding their needs, values, and intrinsic motivators, and appealing to each person's particular worldview and leadership preferences.

Execution & Performance

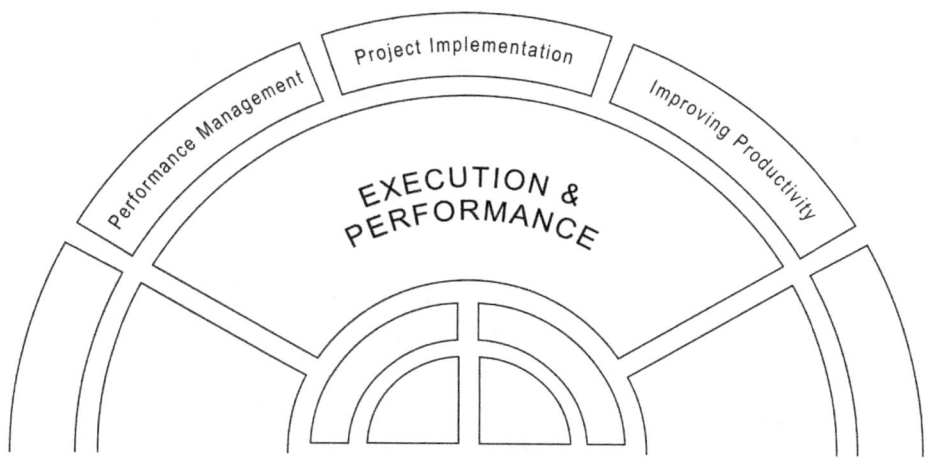

In our first pass, I called this area of responsibility and this "essential ability" simply "Executing." I will now introduce a more nuanced term, *"Execution & Performance."*

For review, I defined this area of responsibility as: *guiding productive work to execute the strategy, coordinating work, implementing projects, and managing people's performance.*

Execution & Performance, includes all of the activities related to establishing roles and responsibilities, identifying and closing performance gaps, planning and managing projects using the appropriate tools to coordinate work across teams, and maintaining high productivity so that the organizational resources are used efficiently to achieve shared goals in the desired time frames.

Performance Management

This skill set involves managing performance so that responsibilities, expectations, and agreements are consistently met, including ongoing "accountability conversations" to manage commitments and breakdowns when expectations are not met.

Implementation

This skill set is concerned with planning quarterly and monthly projects, defining objectives, workstreams, tasks and timelines, coordinating the people and activities necessary to stay on track and consistently complete projects on time and on budget.

Productivity

The last skill set is concerned with your ability to help your organization complete work in a productive, organized, efficient and effective way, including managing calendars and tasks, running effective meetings, and staying focused and proactive in the face of distractions, urgencies and obstacles.

Now that we have established a high-level understanding of the nine skill sets that leaders draw upon (at whatever level of ability they currently possess) to fulfill their responsibilities, we can take bold steps toward our goal of rapidly increasing your leadership competency.

To draw again on our previously-used baseball analogy, soon we will enter the "batting cage" to work on our ability to hit the ball. But we have one more important foundation to lay that is necessary for success with an accelerating learning effort. But first, will take a close look at the four universal "follower mindsets" that unequivocally dictate which style of leadership a person will find credible, resonant and will want to follow.

Using the Right Style with the Right Followers

A person's worldview dictates how they see the world, what they believe is true about the world and the people in it, and what they value.

For leaders to be viewed as credible, they must match the correct leadership style with the followers' worldview. This is the key to all "resonant" leadership.

When a leader uses a leadership style that is associated with a worldview different from the follower's, this signals to the follower that this leader "doesn't get it." Put another way, the follower sees the leader as out of touch, clueless, not understanding what is really important, or not getting how the world really works.

A lack of "worldview alignment" results in the follower seeing the leader as not credible, not competent, or in the worst case, not trustworthy.

This is the key to what Ken Wilber and our academic colleagues call "integral leadership" which is another word for integrally-informed leadership, that is, leadership that is informed by integral psychology.

This is one of the main things that sets this leadership development approach apart from most of the other leadership learning methods available in the market.

Our approach to leadership is informed by a nuanced understanding of psychology, in particular, integral psychology which incorporates developmental psychology, worldviews and value systems, all of which are essential for effective leadership.

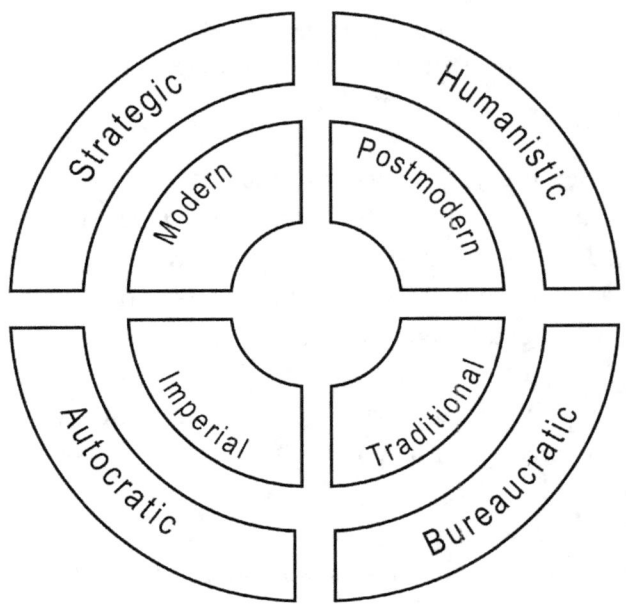

You will recall this diagram from the Universal Leadership Model that shows the four leadership styles lined up with the follower worldviews. This is absolutely essential.

As I have explained, if you use the wrong leadership style with the wrong person you run the risk of destroying your leadership credibility with that person; you will very likely appear clueless and possibly even foolish.

After teaching this unique approach to leadership to thousands of executives in corporate America, I can tell you with experience and authority that this leadership practice of "aligning leadership style with "follower mindsets" has the power to unlock and amplify the potency of the other principles and practices associated with leadership.

Using the correct "leadership style" that matches the follower's (or team's) worldview amplifies the effectiveness of every other technique described in this book and my other on leadership.

"Leadership sensemaking" is most fundamentally about "perspective taking." An integral approach to leadership involves using numerous frameworks as "lenses" which provide visibility into dimensions of reality that conventional leaders are unaware of, overlook, or ignore. The result of these superior (more accurate) lenses and precision perspective-taking practices is greater awareness, better approaches, and more skillful action.

While "matching styles with mindsets" is central to this revolutionary method, it does not represent the totality of it. Rather, it provides a logical and helpful orienting framework—like the conventions of North, South, East, West on a geographical map—to ensure that the leader is headed in the right direction. As you read this section, please be mindful of the fact that this is merely an introduction, a high-level overview of this framework. The goal is for you to become familiar with it. The application of these leadership styles (to all of the different abilities and skill sets) will come with time. It should be obvious that understanding the mindset of your followers (or your team or culture) is central to leadership effectiveness. In fact, most comprehensive leader development programs teach some methods for "understanding people."

Some simply teach listening skills, many teach various kinds of personality typology systems, and a few use stages of development (a.k.a. stages of psychological maturity) to help leaders better understand their followers and what makes them tick.

I'm going to use an American idiom—being "in the ballpark"—as an analogy to illustrate a crucial point. Those personality types, situational leadership tactics, and get-to-know-your-people methods are like finding your section and seat at a large baseball game.

Assuming that you are in the correct stadium, knowing the exact section, row and seat number is very helpful. But here's the catch. In this analogy, your followers' worldview (their values and universal beliefs) represents the stadium. If you fail to accurately recognize your followers' worldview, then you are not even in the right ballpark; therefore, the details about personality types and behavioral tendencies (even a person's goals) are essentially useless.

Worldview is the overall perspective from which one sees and interprets the world.

> *A person's worldview defines what they care about, what motivates them, what they believe is worthwhile, and what they believe lacks value or is "wrong." And as we now understand it also specifically dictates which leadership style they will be resonant with, and follow, as well as which approaches are likely to backfire.*

If you want to understand people, you first need to get "into the right ballpark" by identifying their worldview.

I believe that the failure to grasp meaning making systems—what I am calling worldviews here—lies at the heart of the problem with conventional approaches to leadership. Those approaches often wrongly assume that people's motivations are homogenous. Most conventional approaches to leadership (and also management) fail to adequately take into account the fact that people with different worldviews value different things, interpret the same facts differently, and subsequently have very different priorities. This mistake is at the heart of the "bogus leadership advice" most so-called experts offer.

Follower Mindsets Are the Key to Leadership Success

I mentioned Barbara Kellerman (author of *Bad Leadership, The End of Leadership* and *Professionalizing Leadership*) and Jeffrey Pfeffer (author of *Leadership BS)* in the introduction. Unfortunately, these two courageous "whistleblowers" are among only a few leadership experts that are acknowledging the fact that most leadership development programs focus mainly on the leader and generally ignore "context" in which the leadership is occurring. Worse, they almost all leave the followers out of the equation altogether.

Yes, you read that right. The majority of leadership training programs mostly or completely ignore the followers!

They focus the vast majority of the time talking about traits of great leaders and qualities of effective leaders with seemingly no awareness at all of the needs, worldviews and preferences of the followers. This, again, is one of the main reasons that most leadership development programs produce such criminally dismal results. In her books, Kellerman really takes the leadership industry to talk over this colossal error. She underscores the fact that any legitimate approach to leadership must take into account all three elements of the leader, the context (the circumstances), and especially the followers.

I would suggest that one of the most important aspects of a leader's context or circumstances, is their follower's worldviews. If you understand the follower's worldview (or mindset, then you will know what they care about, what is important to them, how they define leadership, and what they look for in a person they view as a credible leader.

Most importantly, if you know a person's "follower mindset," and you know how to match up the mindsets with the four Universal Leadership Styles, then you can avoid the embarrassing situation of using the wrong style with the wrong person and destroying your leadership credibility in their eyes.

In the same way that beauty is in the eye of the beholder, leadership is in the eye of the follower. If you use the wrong leadership style with the wrong person they will not see you as a credible leader. They will see you as clueless or even foolish. A leadership approach that is extremely resonant with one employee, team or department will be ineffective or even offensive for another. The troublesome issue is:

"How can you know which approach will be effective and which will be offensive?"

The answer, of course, is the follower's worldview.

As I mentioned in the section about the Leadership Rosetta Stone, integral psychology shows us that about 95% of the values/belief systems that today's leaders are likely to encounter fall into four broad worldviews.

For some readers, this fact is not new. Many readers are already familiar with Modern, Postmodern, and Traditional worldviews. However, few people are aware of the fact that these "value systems" predict with astonishing accuracy which leadership style will be resonant and appreciated, and which styles will be met with resistance and/or rejection.

It is hard to overstate the significance of this. This realization lies at the heart of the breakthrough that my team discovered, with Ken Wilber's guidance in the early 2000s. Essentially, this deceptively simple Universal Leadership Model successfully aggregates, synthesizes, and integrates, more than a 100 years of leadership theories.

Moreover, once sufficiently internalized in practice (and that takes a little time of course), this unique leadership framework allows leaders to effectively motivate and influence followers (of all kinds) with a level of precision and efficacy that is rarely witnessed.
Also, this works everywhere it has been tested. In corporate environments, financial services, construction sites, assembly lines, hospitals, police forces, military... even in remote African tribal villages.

Values Research

Worldviews are composed of values and universal beliefs. Values are perceptual filters minds use to determine ("evaluate") what is important in any given situation. Universal beliefs are broad-based beliefs about self, others, and system (how the world is perceived to work). In terms of knowing which leader a given person is likely to follow (or elect given the choice), in terms of knowing what people care about, in terms of knowing what motivates people, in terms of understanding people in the most fundamental sense, nothing is more germane than values.

The conceptualization and use of values models is widespread and informed by a multitude of different approaches that differ in details but are quite similar in principle and overarching conclusions. Values research is widely used by psychologists, political scientists, and marketers. The pervasive role of values in all aspects of human life has motivated hundreds of studies in the disciplines of psychology, sociology, cultural anthropology, and consumer behavior.

A large body of research has shown conclusively that values represent both a powerful explanation of and influence on a variety of individual and collective behaviors. In fact, in recent years, the study and measurement of values has become one of the most dynamic research areas in the social science disciplines (management, leadership, marketing and consumer behavior). Several values measurement methodologies are currently available and more are surfacing.

These worldviews, along with their correlating universal leadership styles, cut across nationalities, ethnicity, and culture. There is nothing inherently American or North American (or European or Caucasian) about these worldviews and leadership styles. However, I live in the U.S. and most of my work has involved leaders in the Americas. The examples and illustrations in my teaching reflect my experience.

Also, in this presentation, I often use the term "mindset" in place of or in addition to the more academic term "worldview."

When describing people who hold a worldview, it is often helpful to use the word "mindset" in place of the word worldview. Rather than say, this person holds a modern worldview, we could say, this person has a "modern mindset" or better still, this person has an "achiever mindset." This section of the book will follow this convention and will use "mindset" in place of "worldview." This presentation uses broad and simplified examples of single worldviews or mindsets that help new students become familiar with their basic appearance and function. Once you can begin to recognize them, in time you will begin to see how they can be combined (as some people's mindset is a blend of two such as 50/50 or 60/40).

Next, I will go through each of the four follower mindsets, describe how the world looks through that lens, refer to the massive amount of research that backs up these assertions, and give you several examples of "profiles" of employees who typify this mindset. After the explanation of the follower mindset, then I will offer a more detailed explanation of the style of leadership that should be used with people with that mindset.

Achiever Mindset

People with a modern worldview can also be described as having an "Achiever mindset." They identify with being highly rational, competitive, ambitious, autonomous and elite. They emphasize success and/or status as defined by material acquisition and "upward mobility."

They value excellence, advancement, prosperity, achievement, and status. Most importantly, they prefer to follow leaders who are perceived to have the most expertise and ability to achieve goals. In other words, they follow leaders who use the Strategic Leadership style.

The Achiever mindset (and the Strategic Leadership style) is well suited for the following environments and circumstances: sales departments, professional services firms, innovation-driven organizations, senior management positions, and in roles that require advanced levels of education such as scientific research.

Seeing the World Through an Achiever's Lens

In academic circles, this worldview is referred to as the "Modern worldview" (as contrasted to the Traditional and Postmodern worldviews).

When you look at the world through this lens, you see a playing field full of possibilities to explore and opportunities to achieve. You will emphasize the scientific and rational dimensions of what you see. The key to life is to strive for, and achieve "success."

Through this lens, it becomes easy to believe in the advancement of humankind through the application of the highly disciplined rational mind and its scientific, technological, and medical manifestations. Life is to be met and mastered by finding the best way to act on its limitless opportunities.

Empirical Research

While this worldview, or "follower mindset" may be new for a few readers, there is nothing new, novel or controversial about it; in fact, my descriptions are based on widely-accepted and respected empirical research that has come out of Harvard, Yale, Boston College, Washington University and other top institutions over the last four decades. I offer more nuanced, academic analysis in other books (especially my book series on Integral Leadership). For this introduction, I will mention the academic terms that the different leading psychologists use for this worldview / follower mindset. McClelland uses the term "Achievement," Loevinger uses "Conscientious," Kohlberg uses "Social Order," Graves uses

"Multiplistic-Achievist," Kegan uses "Institutional," Wade uses "Achievement," and Torbert uses "Achiever." When I'm using "follower mindset" terminology, I say Achiever mindset and when I'm using the worldview term, I call it the Modern worldview. Although I don't use Ken Wilber's color schemes in this book series created for mainstream readers, for my readers who are students of integral theory, I will mention here that the Wilberian color code for this worldview is "orange."

Understanding People with an Achiever Mindset

People with this mindset tend to believe that while there are many valid ways to think and behave, there is always one best way. People with this mindset want to feel they are at the "top of their game" and that they have earned (quite literally, in some cases) the recognition of belonging to an elite group.

They are not satisfied to simply "play by the rules;" rather, they want to fully understand the rules to gain a competitive advantage over those with less acuity, with the ultimate ambition of becoming so successful that they might eventually "change the rules of the game." Many of their decisions will be motivated by the promise of success and status, as well as an awareness and fairly sophisticated understanding of the dynamics of the overall system within which they operate (company, church, nation, global marketplace).

Some examples of occupational roles that tend to epitomize the Achiever mindset include salespeople, attorneys, research scientists, marketing agents, PR and advertising representatives, elected public officials, architects, and physicians in conventional practice (as opposed to alternative medicine which would very likely be someone with a Pluralistic mindset described in the next section). Following are some example profiles of people with these mindsets.

Rob - Research Scientist

I'm a research scientist who's convinced that most of the world's problems can be solved with the right technological advancements and tools. I think that many people hold superstitious, irrational beliefs that are detrimental to society's interests and retard scientific progress. While I enjoy my work during the week, I pursue my real passion on the weekends. I've completed over twenty triathlons and placed in the top five in most of them. My training schedule could probably qualify as some sort of third world form of punishment, but when I cross the finish line in first place it's all worth it. There's a force in me that's relentless in its determination to win. There's something exhilarating about testing your limits and pushing your personal edge.

Danielle - Attorney

I just graduated from Harvard Law School and I am joining one of the most prestigious firms in the country. I grew up in a two-parent working class household and was a latch-key kid. My parents were focused on providing necessities for us. They helped me to see that hard work and determination are keys to success. While I respect my parents "traditional" ways, I knew from a young age that I wanted to work smarter, not harder, to enjoy the finer things in life. And while my parents' religious orientation works for them, I wasn't satisfied with simplistic answers to complex questions. To be honest, I believe that the world would be a better place if more people would put their faith in reason and look to science rather than religion for answers.

Lee - Small Business Owner

I own a small web-based company that produces and sells custom laptop cases for the fashion-conscious consumer. As a start-up, I wasn't entirely sure what I was doing but decided to take some calculated risks while telling myself that failing wasn't an option. I became incredibly focused and goal-oriented, and within two years I was featured as Entrepreneur of the Year in a nation-wide magazine.

Strategic Leadership

People like Lee, Danielle and Rob who have an Achiever worldview prefer to follow leaders who embody personal excellence and success and who are perceived to be most likely to achieve predefined goals.

In this form of leadership, the person with the most expertise leads via strategic planning and tangible incentives. It is characterized by incentivizing teams to execute well-conceived plans to outperform their competitors. In academic terms, this approach is sometimes referred to as "transactional" to differentiate it from the "transformational" quality of the Collaborative Leadership style.

It's easy to see how the Achiever mindset finds this strategic, goal-oriented leadership approach resonant.

In fact, as we shall see, the developers and advocates of the many "schools of leadership" that fall into this category nearly always possess the corresponding worldview.

This explains why academics / researchers / authors who are enthusiastic proponents of each leadership style believe that their style is the best and should be used in every situation.

When you are with a group of people who share the same values system, if you pay attention to their language, you will notice that they have a way of communicating with each other that reflects their common values and beliefs.

My mentor Ken Wilber refers to this as the "Dominant Mode of Discourse." I use the shorter term "Values Dialect" (or simply dialect). This values dialect is the dialect of business.

Leaders whose primary mindset is Affiliative or Traditional who want to be taken seriously in business need to learn to speak the Achiever dialect even if it is not their "native tongue."

Affiliative Mindset

People with an affiliative mindset identify with being nonjudgmental, egalitarian, and socially and environmentally conscious.

They value connection, tolerance, cultural sensitivity, diversity, sustainability, and interdependence. They strive for fulfillment as defined by personal growth, increased awareness, harmonious relationships, and "making a difference."

Most importantly, they prefer to follow leaders who are perceived as being aware, sensitive to the wellbeing of others, value consensus, and always treat others as equals; in other words, leaders who use a Humanistic leadership style. My colleagues and I also refer to this style as the "Collaborative" leadership style. I will use both terms in this book series.

Seeing the World Through an Affiliative Lens

In academic circles, this worldview is referred to as the "Postmodern Worldview" (as opposed to the Modern or Traditional). It is sometimes also called a "pluralistic" worldview.

Sociologist and bestselling author Paul Ray uses the term "Cultural Creatives" to describe people who identify with the worldview. In his book *The Cultural Creatives: How 50 Million People Are Changing the World*, he summarizes research on 50 million adult Americans (slightly over one quarter of the adult population). Ray presents a significant amount of demographic and psychographic research comparing and contrasting this worldview to the Traditional worldview and Modern worldview.

When you look at the world through this Postmodern or "pluralistic" lens, you see a diverse ecosystem where cooperation leads to synergy.

The dictionary definition of pluralistic is: "a social perspective that believes no single explanatory system or view of reality can account for all the phenomena of life; rather there are many (plural) truths. Further, it is desirable to have numerous distinct ethnic, religious, or cultural groups present and tolerated in society."

Empirical Research

My descriptions in this book are all based on empirical research out of Harvard, Yale, Boston College, Washington University and other top institutions over the last four decades. For this introduction, I will mention the academic terms that the different leading psychologists use for this worldview / follower mindset. McClelland uses the term "Affiliative," Loevinger uses "Individualistic," Kohlberg uses "Social Contract," Graves uses "Relativistic-Personalistic," Kegan uses "late-institutional" into "early-Interindividual," Wade uses "Affiliative," and Torbert uses "Individualist." Although I don't use Ken Wilber's color schemes in this book series created for mainstream readers, for my readers who are students of integral theory, I will mention here that the Wilberian color code for this worldview is "green."

Understanding People with an Affiliative Mindset

Historically, leaders with the postmodern worldview and Affiliative mindset were responsible for the human rights and environmental movements.

People with this mindset tend to display egalitarian, tolerant attitudes, and are often enthusiastic endorsers of equal rights and equal opportunity for all people in all situations. People with this mindset want to feel as though they are "making a difference."

Their decisions tend to be motivated by the belief that their choice will help them (or their organization) continue to grow and develop, and that the world will be positively impacted (or at least not negatively affected) by their actions.

Whereas, people with the Achiever mindset emphasize external/material accomplishments (financial success, material acquisitions, status), people with this Affiliative mindset prefer to emphasize internal/intangible accomplishments (awareness, human connection, emotional fulfillment).

As such, they are more motivated by personal growth, people, and relationships than by material gain.

Of course this group can be highly motivated to achieve material success for a social or environmental cause as long as this is accomplished without sacrifices of personal growth or rewarding relationships.

People with this mindset gravitate toward communities that value tolerance for multiple perspectives, interdependence, creativity, diversity, activism, and "progressive" approaches.

They prefer nontraditional, "humanized" workplaces where self-expression is encouraged and rewarded; where contribution to social, political, and environmental causes is mission-critical or intrinsic to profitability; where duties and roles are actively interchanged in the service of a nonhierarchical, egalitarian approach; where team and roundtable gatherings are standard to internal operations and decision-making; where the job requires higher education; and where ongoing growth and development along with "work-life-balance" are encouraged. Following, I provide some profiles of people with this Affiliative mindset. I am certain one of these profiles (if not more than one) will remind you of someone you know. Pay attention to these patterns, they are all around you, and the sooner you begin to recognize them, the sooner you will know which leadership style or approach will be resonant with them.

Jonathan - Volunteer

Right out of college I joined the Peace Corps. At some point during my senior year, I realized that most of the world's population will never have the opportunities I once took for granted. Today, I work as a diversity consultant in the public sector, I help people within organizations accept and find strength in each others' differences. There's a real tendency in all of us to feel that our own way of looking at things is intrinsically superior, and it's this attitude that is responsible for most of the world's conflict. If everyone would accept each other's differences, we'd finally have a peaceful planet.

Delia - Record Label Owner

At eighteen, I founded my own music label because I wanted to promote social justice and retain artistic integrity that a corporate mentality wouldn't allow. After selling over 50,000 of my albums, the major labels came courting with huge deals. Because they wanted me to compromise, I declined. Today, my label is an internationally known icon for independent art, political action, and grassroots sponsorship.

Larry - Physician

I'm an MD and the founder of a holistic health care company that's committed to people and the planet first and profit second. I've taken great care to give everyone in my organization an equal voice; there is no hierarchy to speak of, and decision-making is done by consensus. As far as I'm concerned, a good business should function a lot like a democracy to ensure that too much power isn't invested in any one person. It's clear to me that the modern lifestyle being commercialized and relentlessly promoted by megacorporations is environmentally unsustainable for the planet. When I recognized I was part of the problem, I decided to become part of the solution by simplifying my life and limiting my consumption.

Humanistic Leadership

People like Larry, Delia and Jonathon who have an Affiliative mindset prefer to follow leaders who are perceived as being aware, sensitive to the wellbeing of others, value consensus, and treat others as equals. People with the Affiliative mindset believe that leadership is not vested in any single person; rather, it should be consensus-based in the sense that self-managed teams should lead themselves.

This approach is considered "transformational" and involves inviting people's perceptions, feelings and intuition via roundtable discussion and dialog to arrive at consensus, then work collaboratively toward common goals that serve the greater good. It is also called "Collaborative" leadership. Leadership is also likely to be understood as situational and temporary; nearly all position-based authority is therefore highly questionable or even rejected outright. Unlike the Traditional mindset, people with the Affiliative mindset abhor hierarchy and will tend to either ignore it or seek to actively undermine it.

Many of the books that promote work-life balance, emotionally-aware "resonant" leadership, and "appreciative inquiry" are both popular with people having a Affiliative mindset and were written by people with Affiliative mindsets. Katzenbach and Smith's bestselling book, *The Wisdom of Teams,* was mentioned earlier in the leadership theory section of this book.

When authors are subject to their own worldview (and fail to recognize the different worldviews at play in the workplace), they tend to advocate their approach as the best approach. This is another example of the rampant unconscious worldview bias that we see in this field of leadership development.

In fact, it is Humanistic leadership (also called "transformational leadership" or "collaborative leadership") that is currently in the vanguard of popular business literature. For many leaders, this humanistic, transformational approach is a welcome shift away from the transactional and traditional (bureaucratic) approaches that have been popular for so long. However, sophisticated leaders see the flaw in this thinking. There is no best leadership approach for all types of people. The best leadership approach is the one that will be most resonant with the people you hope to lead.

Humanistic leadership works great with people with Affiliative mindsets. However, people with an Achiever mindset consider it to be too touchy-feely, people with a Traditional mindset consider its relativistic values to be immoral, and people with a Power mindset interpret kindness and sensitivity as weaknesses and steamroll right over it.

Traditional Mindset

People with a Traditional Mindset identify with being responsible, purposeful, and self-sacrificing. They seek a reassuring sense of stability, security, and belonging by conforming to a worldview that they unambiguously describe as the tried and true "natural order of things."

This natural order of things is defined by the long-standing traditions of the culture in which they were socialized. As you would expect, people with this mindset prefer to follow leaders who are perceived as having positional and/or moral authority; in other words, leaders who use an Authoritarian Leadership style.

Seeing the World Through a Traditional Lens

You no doubt recognize that this is what academics refer to as the "Traditional worldview" (contrasting it with the familiar Modern and Postmodern Worldviews).

When you look through this Traditional lens, you see an ordered existence under the control of a higher authority and ultimate Truth.

Although amber is the integral theory color code we associate with this worldview, when you look through the lens, what you actually see is black-and-white.

People who use this lens to view the world perceive a concrete, literal, dualistic world of right and wrong, insiders and outsiders, believers and non-believers, and good and evil. They also see people who conform to rigid traditional roles (such as man earning money and women staying home and raising children) as following the "natural order of things" and people who deviate from conventional roles (such as people who are gender fluid, non-binary or identify as trans) as aberration at best and evil at worst.

If you know what to look for it is very easy to spot people with this Traditional mindset.

Empirical Research

My descriptions are all based on empirical research from Harvard, Yale, Boston College, Washington University and other top institutions over the last four decades. For this introduction, I will mention the academic terms that the different leading psychologists use for this worldview / follower mindset. McClelland uses the term "Authority," Loevinger uses "Conformist," Kohlberg uses "Interpersonal Accord" and "Conformity," Graves uses "Absolutistic-Obedience," Kegan uses "Interpersonal," Wade uses "Conformist," and Torbert uses "Diplomat."

When I'm using "follower mindset" terminology, I say Traditional mindset and Traditional worldview. Although I don't use Ken Wilber's color schemes in this book series created for mainstream readers, for my readers who are students of integral theory, I will mention here that the Wilberian color code for this worldview is "amber." Also some readers may be familiar with the National Values Center / Spiral Dynamics colors, which is "blue" for this mindset.

Understanding People with a Traditional Mindset

People with Traditional mindsets tend to be dedicated, reliable, loyal, responsible, conscientious, and can be expected to think and act in routine, predictable ways.

They are oriented around learning and following the rules defined by authority, and are more than willing to subjugate their own impulses and desires in the service of a greater calling, cause, or mission that they find meaningful, purposeful and in accord with their traditional beliefs.

While "Blue Collar jobs" are typical, people with this mindset are especially attracted to work that promotes what they consider to be the moral good (e.g., ministers, teachers, police officers, guidance counselors, children's athletic coaches, etc.). In addition to preferring jobs that require routine and discipline, this group thrives in circumstances that others might view as repetitive or tedious. Consequently, they excel in standards and compliance roles as well as organizational and system maintenance jobs.

People with this Traditional mindset value hierarchy; therefore, they respond best to clearly defined rules, deadlines, responsibilities and a well-defined chain of command. They also appreciate a written code of conduct to refer to, especially one that offers clear protocols for action and predictable consequences for success and failure.

Wherever in the world you encounter the Traditional worldview, it will define acceptable and unacceptable gender roles, sexual orientations and practices, food and drink consumption, and of course spiritual practices based on the long-standing traditions endemic to the culture they were raised in.

For people with this Traditional mindset, there is one and only one right way to think and behave. Conforming to authority's prescribed "right" way to think and behave is the key to ensure future rewards.

It is very important to understand that while the details of the local customs and culture (including religious practices) will differ, the broad-based core values and universal beliefs that comprise a Traditional worldview will be identical anywhere on the planet, whether it be Tehran, Turkey, Thailand or West Texas.

As an integrally-informed leader, you must understand that in Traditional cultures, both Modern and Postmodern values tend to be viewed not only with skepticism and suspicion, but often with fear and in some cases, hatred.

Fear is a major motivator underlying a feeling of "us vs. them" in the form of a common enemy that threatens the traditional way of life of the traditional lifestyle.

Proponents of the Traditional worldview (regardless of country or culture) understand these drives inherently and use positional or perceived moral authority to galvanize loyalty and motivate followers (or perhaps to gain views and viewers or sell books).

In the U.S., books such as Sean Hannity's *Deliver Us from Evil* and Bill O'Reilly's *Culture Warrior* make a convincing case that Modern and Postmodern values are a dangerous threat to the traditional way of life. So do Ann Coulter's books and Tucker Carlson's talk show episodes. These are all good examples of this fear and hatred of worldviews that deviate from the traditional view and traditional lifestyle.

The traditional mindset is based on a "parental orientation" to reality that is binary, there are parents and children and not much in between.

The leader is a parental figure and the followers are like children who should obey. The leader is seen as the authority. This is why in leadership theory, it is referred to as "authoritarian" leadership. For the traditional mindset, the authority (who is in the position of parent) should tell the followers (who are in the position of children) how to work, succeed, be moral, and generally live a good life (according to God's plan or according to the "one true way").

> *To an individual who holds this Traditional worldview, the person that has been annointed, appointed or elected is the de facto leader.*

People with a traditional mindset view leadership as "positional." So the "Minister" and the "Mayor" are the defacto leaders.

There is one very important exception to this principle.

If the appointed or elected person does not share their traditional values and beliefs, then they will be rejected. This is very important to understand.

In this scenario, the elected leader is viewed as *illegitimate, a fake, a fraud,* or an *opportunist* who is only doing it for egocentric gain, and should be removed from that position as quickly as possible, in some cases, by any means necessary!

This reliably explains and predicts the right-wing behavior toward elected leaders viewed as "liberals."

Perhaps there is no better example of this than how the United States traditional values voters reacted to the election of Barack Obama. They (with rare exceptions) despised him, because they fear and often hate leaders that do not share their traditional values and beliefs. We saw this again when Joe Biden was elected as U.S. president.

Note that I said "that they believe" follow their traditional values. Unfortunately it is not difficult for actual opportunists (a.k.a. "autocrats") who do <u>not</u> actually have traditional beliefs to convince gullible traditional voters that they do share their traditional beliefs in order to win their support or their votes.

This is why it is very common for traditional voters to vote against their own best interests and to elect politicians who are actually just manipulating them.

Following, I will share some profiles of stereotypical traditional mindset followers. I'm sure you will recognize one or all three of these profiles as employees, colleagues, or perhaps members of your family. Try to look for those patterns.

Once you learn to recognize these mindsets in others, you will know exactly which of the four universal leadership styles they will find resonant, will trust and will willingly follow and for whom they will offer their discretionary effort.

Recall earlier, I said that if you use the wrong leadership style with the wrong follower, they will not see you as credible, worse, they may see you as clueless or even foolish.

Here is a real-life example of that principle in action.

If you use a Humanistic leadership style (a.k.a. collaborative, transformational or "self-managed teams") with one of these people, it will destroy your credibility in their eyes. They will see you as just "not getting it" (that is you don't get how the world really is). And they may see you as clueless, or even foolish.

So as you read about John, Susan and Daniel on the following pages, use this opportunity to find your followers in these descriptions!

John - True Believer

It's true, I've been called "straight laced" more than once. But people who know the Truth have a duty to defend it, even if it means being politically incorrect. People talk about "shades of gray" but as far as I'm concerned, right is right and wrong is wrong. Ultimately, almost everything is black and white, and those who suggest otherwise are just avoiding moral responsibility.

Susan - School Counselor

I love God, my family, and my country—in that order. I'm particularly proud of my nationality—when I hear people criticizing the leaders of my country I tend to feel rather insulted and often angry. I really feel that some things are simply not ours to question, and that obedience and loyalty are the highest virtues to which a person can aspire for. I work as a school counselor. I'm sometimes baffled why so many of today's kids go to such great lengths to be "different." By striving to be such "non-conformists" they don't fit in. Also, I feel frustrated by our school's tolerance for modes of dress and conduct that I find socially unacceptable and are against the family values that all schools should reinforce.

Daniel - Faith-Based Counselor

I teach a vocational rehab class for single parents and one of the things I stress to my students is that if you follow the rules—both in my class and life in general—you're bound to come out all right. With the world as unpredictable as it is, it just doesn't pay to take many risks or deviate from what's been proven to work. What is most important is having stability and knowing that you and those you love will have a secure future.

Authority Leadership

People like John, Susan and Daniel who have a Traditional worldview prefer to follow leaders they perceive as having positional or moral authority, who share their traditional beliefs, and who lead using strict adherence to a "chain of command" or the "rules" of the institution that has bestowed that authority. In other words, people with traditional mindsets see the "Bureacratic" leader (also called "Authoritarian" leader) as the most credible, legitimate and trustworthy leaders.

This term, "authoritarian leadership," is, in fact, the well-researched, widely- acknowledged and accurate academic term for this authority-centric style of leadership.

For corporate audiences, especially ones that are composed of a lot of traditionalists, the term "Bureaucratic leadership" is preferred. I will use both terms in this book.

In this leadership style, the person with *positional authority* leads via chain of command. This approach is "Hierarchical" and is characterized by compliance with the rules to meet the requirements dictated by the person with authority.

While fear and guilt are primary motivators for people with a Traditional mindset, they do not want their leaders to show either of these emotions. Effective authoritarian leaders (Bureaucratic leaders) intuit this and rarely, if ever, admit they don't know something or admit when they have made a mistake, or admit they are afraid.

That kind of "vulnerability based self-disclosure works will Humanistic leadership with followers with an Affiliative mindset, but authoritarian / bureaucratic leaders (with Traditional followers) rarely if ever admit their mistakes, their lack of knowledge or their fears, doubts or uncertainties.

George W. Bush, a well-known authoritarian leader, understood this implicitly as he is having a "Traditional" mindset and his native style is authoritarian (also called Bureaucratic." In his eight years as President of the United States, even in the face of incontrovertible evidence of poor judgment and costly errors (financial, military, international affairs, many millions of unnecessary deaths and so on), he never admitted making mistakes.

While many have criticized this behavior, to his credit, this was exactly what his large base of "traditional values voters" wanted to see in their leader.

People with other mindsets tend to view this trait as an inability to admit mistakes or learn from them, yet people with this Traditional mindset will describe this same behavior as "principled."

Using the same Traditional lens, popular leadership authors and theorists (including many "leadership experts") write books about the innate "character traits of leaders," the enduring "laws of leadership," or the "steps to being a great leader."

Author John Maxwell's bestselling books are excellent examples of the traditional view of leadership.

While Modern and Postmodern writers criticize what they consider to be reductionist approaches to life and leadership, it is very important to remember that advocates of this worldview (such Tucker Carlson, Glenn Beck, Sean Hannity, Ann Coulter) are so popular precisely because a large percentage of the population (estimated 40% in the U.S.) have adopted this Traditional worldview.

Integrally-informed leadership is concerned with seeing the world as it actually is and meeting people in it as they actually are. Integrally-informed leaders realize that although the Authoritarian / Bureaucratic leadership style may lack a certain nuance as compared to other styles, it is exactly the approach that a very large percentage of the population is most resonant with.

Power Mindset

Previously, I used the word "Imperial" to describe this worldview. As mentioned previously, worldviews are a psychological and somewhat academic term. For corporate audiences, we often pivot to "mindset" terminologies to offer a more user-friendly vernacular.

Here, when describing people who hold this worldview, I will introduce a new term, the "Power-Centric Mindset" or "Power Mindset" for short.

People with a Power mindset identify with being strong, courageous risk takers, who are capable of defending themselves in a dangerous world and getting what they want, when they want it.

They emphasize personal power as defined by the ability to live outside conventional rules and gratify their desires. They value power, protection, freedom, respect, and control. Most importantly, they prefer to follow leaders who are perceived as being the strongest, toughest, and most dominant; in other words, leaders who use an Autocratic Leadership style.

Seeing the World Through a Power-Centric Lens

Academics refer to this worldview as the "Imperial worldview". It's easy to see this worldview dominating many periods of human history. You have probably heard it described as "Machiavellian."

This term derives from the book The Prince written in 1513 by Niccolo Machiavelli as a pragmatic guide to getting and keeping power in a dangerous world. In The Prince, Machiavelli famously advocates "the ends justify the means." This pretty much sums up the Imperial worldview and the Autocratic Leadership style that is best paired with it.

When you look at the world through this Power-centric lens, you see a jungle filled with predators and selfcentered people, where only the strongest and most cunning survive and thrive.

If this is your world, or at least your worldview, you tend to view others as competitors for scarce resources and will tend to interpret hesitation, softness, or even kindness, as signs of weakness.

From this point of view, team members are useful allies in the ongoing quest for power and when a common enemy is identified, the team can marshal its resources quite effectively.

To this worldview, "might" really does make "right."

The "haves" deserve their status and privilege because they are powerful and dominant, and the "have not's" deserve their status because of their weakness or incompetence. Above all, people with the Power mindset value power and respect, and will respond favorably only to leaders who are perceived to be powerful and who "command respect."

Empirical Research

My descriptions in this book are all based on empirical research out of Harvard, Yale, Boston College, Washington University and other top institutions. For this introduction, I will mention the academic terms that the different leading psychologists use for this worldview / follower mindset. McClelland uses the term "Power," Loevinger uses "Self-Protective," Kohlberg uses "Self-Interest," Graves uses "Egocentric-Exploitive," Kegan uses "Imperial," Wade uses "Egocentric," and Torbert uses "Opportunist."

When I'm using "follower mindset" terminology, I say Power mindset and when I'm using the worldview term, I call it the Imperial worldview. Although I don't use Ken Wilber's color schemes in this book series created for mainstream readers, for my readers who are students of integral theory, I will mention here that the Wilberian color code for this worldview is "red."

Understanding People with a Power Mindset

People who identify with the Power mindset tend to be persuasive, egocentric, courageous, impulsive, and often charismatic. People with this mindset play crucial roles in society: the need for people who possess great courage and inner strength, and are willing to take enormous risks. However, people with this mindset are not always appreciated, because they also tend to be fiercely independent—"I live by my rules alone" and are disinterested in conforming to the status quo (including many societal norms). They have a tendency to think mainly of themselves and can be insensitive to others' needs and desires in their own uncompromising push to break free from limits, satisfy their desires, or impose their will.

Although both the Power and Achiever mindsets are driven to "win" or "dominate", the "Achiever" drive is fueled by excellence / competitiveness / status while the Power mindset is motivated by power / respect / glory. The Imperial worldview and this Power mindset can be found in every socioeconomic system, but may be more readily noticeable in inner cities and in isolated rural areas.

It is common to encounter people with this mindset in tough environments such as reform schools, heavy construction, oil and gas refineries, and prisons. These are the life conditions that give rise to and reward Power mindsets. Oftentimes people with a Power mindset were raised in or spent many years in these life conditions. When they move on to new circumstances they may carry that worldview with them. As you would expect, people with this mindset gravitate toward social groups that value toughness, aggression, and physical prowess and that encourage behavior sometimes considered "beneath social norms."

Following are profiles of people with a Power mindset. As with the other profiles I have provided in this book, please use these as archetypes and think about how these profiles remind you of some of the people in your life, or perhaps former bosses or co-workers.

People with this Power mindset do not respond well to "Strategic" leadership, to "Collaborative" (or "Humanistic") leadership, or to the parental "Authoritarian" (or Bureaucratic) style of leadership. Followers with this mindset only respect Autocratic leadership. So it is important that you recognize this mindset by seeing the patterns that I am providing you in these profiles.

Mike - Bouncer

I grew up in a tougher part of town—maybe that explains why I've always felt most comfortable in situations where it's "do or die." I did well in school but was bored with it. I dropped out of college and worked as a bouncer for a few years. I enjoyed it but I wanted to make money, so I parlayed my intellect, instinct, and charisma into a successful career in mergers and acquisitions. It's a ruthless business well-suited for me—I was never shy about drawing blood. I work hard and play hard. I generally stay out of trouble though I have had a few close calls. Ask my friends and they'll tell you there's never a dull moment.

Jill - Conservative Talk Radio Host

I've hosted my own radio show for about five years now. It's a tough gig, but fortunately, I enjoy a game of hardball. Though I'm charismatic, I'm known for going for the jugular and being able to verbally dominate a caller, even if their argument is better than mine. Basically, I operate on the premise that if somebody's not strong enough to hold their own with me, they don't deserve much respect.

Sheila - Server

I learned a long time ago that power leads to getting what you want, and that a woman with sex appeal has power over most men. Today, I'm a waitress in one of the most exclusive clubs in town. I basically make a killing by pouring on the nice and, when necessary, flashing a bit of skin. But it's not just about the money, I like the feeling that I'm in control. And I like working in an atmosphere where people aren't concerned about anything but having a good time.

Autocratic Leadership

People like Sheila, Mike and Jill with this Power-centric mindset only willingly follow leaders who they respect, and they do not respect weakness.

Therefore, they tend to follow leaders who are perceived as having the most power, in other words, leaders who use an Autocratic Leadership style. Power-centric followers are motivated by power and respect, not by "people skills."

The Autocratic approach to leadership is "Unilateral" and can be summed up as follows: *impose one's will through reputation, fear and respect, tightly control information and choices, reward compliance and punish disloyalty.*

Try to recall how the world appears through the lens of an Imperial worldview.

If you perceive the world as a jungle or battlefield, then you are likely to believe the best way to advance toward your goals is always to protect yourself, gain power, and outmaneuver others who are perceived as either obedient loyalists or as obstacles, enemies or threats. Note that for autocratic leaders, both the obedient loyalists and the enemies are seen as objects to be manipulated.

If you read any of the numerous books written by former Donald Trump employees (about the man's leadership style) you will discover a textbook-accurate description of this Autocratic leadership approach.

As mentioned in an earlier chapter, bookstores are filled with popular titles that advocate this Autocratic leadership style. As I mentioned, these numerous books would not be so popular if there wasn't a market for them. I will remind you of the Stanly Bing books: *What Would Machiavelli Do? The Ends Justify the Meanness* and *Sun Tzu Was a Sissy: Conquer Your Enemies, Promote Your Friends, and Wage the Real Art of War* and the Robert Greene books *The 48 Laws of Power* and *The 50th Law*. Greene writes, "Learning the game of power requires a certain way of looking at the world, a shifting of perspective." From this autocratic perspective, everyone wants power and everyone is in a constant duplicitous game to gain more power at the expense of others.

While this autocratic style can be extremely useful on the battlefield or the oil field, unfortunately, this style has been seen on the rise even in modern countries, even in prominent leadership roles in government.

Many books (and studies) are available that provide a detailed account of the advantages and (huge) disadvantages seen when this style of leadership is deployed outside of the battlefield or oil field. Much carnage ensues.

Another excellent resource for students of Autocratic leadership, especially when it is used in the wrong context, see Harvard's Barbara Kellerman's book, *The Enablers: How Team Trump Flunked the Pandemic and Failed America.* The problem with this autocratic leadership approach is that people for whom the autocratic leadership style is their dominant style tend to be primarily or exclusively concerned with themselves and perhaps their immediate family or shareholders. Autocratic leadership simply does not work very well when those leaders have the responsibility of the wellbeing of a large diverse constituency of people whose welfare rely on wise decision-making that benefits the greater good.

However, we must never lose sight of the fact that people with a Power mindset, like Mike, Sheila and Jill in our profile examples, strongly prefer autocratic leaders.

We saw this in full effect in the United States at "Trump Rallies" in 2016-2020, and we see it anywhere a population of people with imperial worldviews feel unfairly treated and are looking for a "strongman" leader who promises to "defeat their enemies."

Most people reading this book do not have a primary Imperial worldview and therefore may find this Autocratic style of leadership unappealing, or even feel a strong aversion to it. But you must remember, everyone doesn't think like you do. Always remember that people with an Imperial worldview love autocratic leaders. In fact, they see Autocratic leadership as the only legitimate form of leadership.

Let's take a closer look at this and use our newfound "worldview lenses" to see how the other three mindsets view this Autocratic leadership style.

People who primarily identify with the Affiliative mindset (the Postmodern worldview) find the Autocratic style appalling and think such leaders should not be allowed to lead; they should be stripped of power.

People who primarily identify with the Traditional mindset believe these "power-centric" folks have lost their way and need to be "saved." In their mind, what these "lost souls" need is Jesus (or Allah depending on the culture their parents raised them in). This "save the lost souls" mentality is the basis of popular traditional programs such as the "12-Step" recovery programs which are quite useful for power-centric and traditional addicts but really risky for people with modern and postmodern worldviews.

Some Traditionals do vote for autocrats if they believe the autocrats holds their same ethnocentric beliefs, and if they believe the autocrat's claims that he will defeat their enemies. We see this with right-wing "Nationalists" movements wherever they are found. (Many examples of this have been seen in recent years, not only in the United States but also in Europe, Australia and across Asia).

However, the moment that Traditionalists recognize that the self-serving, manipulative autocrat does not actually share their traditional beliefs, they then see the same leader as immoral, and one who should be stripped of power. To invoke our familiar example from recent American history, this was seen when a subset of right-wing Republicans and gullible evangelicals realized that they had been hoodwinked, and instantly transformed from red cap-wearing MAGA loyalists to "Never Trumpers."

What about Achievers? How do they view the Autocratic leadership style?

People who primarily identify with the Achiever mindset consider the Autocratic style to be a bit extreme, but a potentially useful tool for difficult employees or suppliers that won't respond to any other tactics.

Understandably, many new students of integrally-informed approaches to leadership have difficulty imagining themselves using the Autocratic leadership style.

However, the truth is that people who primarily identify with the Power mindset are extremely unlikely to respond to the Strategic, Humanistic or Authoritarian leadership styles.

What do you do if you encounter, or manage, these Power-centric folks?

Integrally-informed leaders understand the importance of recognizing this mindset when they encounter it, and if necessary, drawing upon aspects of the Autocratic style (hopefully in judicial combination with other styles) to connect with, influence and motivate people who only respect this style. In this section, I introduced you to the key concepts of matching leadership styles to follower mindsets. Next, I want to discuss benchmarking.

Benchmarking Leadership Ability

Peter Drucker famously said, "If you can't measure it, you can't manage it." Many of the articles with titles that sound something like "why most leadership development programs fail" include this issue of measurement. Most leadership training companies use a kind of "smoke and mirrors" tactic to suggest that they measure when they actually don't. Do you know what it is?

Rather than measure the actual performance of the leaders (before and after) the training, and compare results or actual outcomes, they run bogus "participant surveys" and simply ask the participants how they "feel" about the training, are the "satisfied" with the training, and do they think they training might "benefit" their leadership. You don't have to be a PhD statistician to see how utterly bogus this approach is. What they do not do is measure actual leadership behaviors (much less leadership outcomes) before and after these programs.

You may wonder if these leadership training companies are being intentionally deceptive?

I do not think so. I've studied this problem and have become convinced that the reason they do not attempt to measure specific leadership behaviors is they <u>do not teach</u> specific leadership behaviors. Further, most leadership trainers and coaches can't even tell you what effective leadership behaviors look like, in fact, many can't even tell you what leaders actually do.

This comes back to the most fundamental problem with leadership development as it is approached today: most leadership development programs do not even recognize that leadership is a technical and complex skill, therefore they do not even attempt to break the skill down into its component parts. In an earlier example, I used basketball (dribbling, passing, shooting rebounding), baseball (batting, throwing, fielding, running the base), playing a musical instrument (notes, scales, chords, chord progressions) and mixed martial arts (wrestling, striking, grappling). Because most leadership coaching and training programs do not recognize the specific abilities, the skill sets, the techniques (behaviors), they do not teach them, and certainly have no way to measure them.

This massive failure of the leadership development industry is one of the things we must "reinvent" if we are to reform this broken $15B (per year) industry (in the U.S. and closer to $50B worldwide).

You are no doubt familiar with the "gap analysis." If we want to improve an ability, we need to have some kind of reliable measurement or benchmark to compare against and to use to develop training methods, content and evaluate progress over time.

To my knowledge, reliable proficiency benchmarks for the main areas of leadership responsibility as well as the essential leadership skills (for each), are not available anywhere beyond this book.

There are some rudimentary assessments available that I don't find adequate. There are also some very sophisticated 360 tools for evaluating leadership psychology that require significant training and an expensive certification to decipher which can be valuable but are not something that individual leaders (such as the readers of this book) can self-administer. To address an important yet unmet need,

I developed the benchmarks for the three "essential leader abilities" and the nine "leadership core competencies" drawn from more than 20,000 hours of experience researching, developing, evaluating, and training thousands of leaders over the last two decades. To keep this book short, I will refer you to my other book *Accelerating Leadership* (or see the Conclusion section of this book for reference of my other books).

Practice Based Leadership

I am revealing to you the exact mechanism that my partners, employees and students have been using for 20+ years to get 3X to 5X better results (in terms of leadership skill improvement) over conventional leadership education practices.

It is this:

> *We teach leadership as a practice made up of concrete, specific discreet techniques. We de-emphasize concepts and we focus on the specific techniques, the practices that lead to skills, that are common to all outstanding leaders. While we do draw on best practices, we contextualize them to make sure we are using the right approach (and leadership style) with the right people and circumstances.*

It begins with treating leadership like yoga, painting, martial arts, dance or any other complex skill that practitioners deliberately practice in a very specific way.

"Deliberate practice" is the method that surgeons, professional athletes, and peak performers use to quickly learn and internalize new skills. We have used it for 20 years, helping leaders rapidly adopt new skills with consistent results.

I can summarize deliberate practice with three main ideas.

1) *You must train "technique"*

To learn a complex skill efficiently, you must isolate the skill and the techniques that make up the skill, set specific goals based on best practices and benchmarks, practice with full attention and push beyond your comfort zone.

2) *You must receive expert mentorship to do the techniques correctly*

This looks like frequent coaching and guidance from people who have mastered the technique and know how to teach it. Facilitators and coaches must be experts in the specific techniques.

3) *You must obtain feedback to calibrate and improve*

This aspect of deliberate practice involves obtaining immediate feedback (from qualified experts) to be able to calibrate and fine tune the technique as you internalize and habitualize it. The first technique has to be correct before layering on the next. And the next has to be correct before layering on the one that follows it.

This is the essence of "Practice-Based Leadership" which is the method that my partners and I pioneered 22 years ago.

I am not going to mince words here. Do not spend another dollar with so-called leadership development experts who aren't experts in the specific techniques of leadership that you need to learn to improve your skills.

You would never hire a guitar teacher or a baseball coach who can't play guitar or who isn't a terrific baseball player (or who doesn't know which techniques to teach you, or who talks about the "qualities" or "traits" of great guitar or baseball players). Don't hire leadership trainers or coaches who do that either!

To break it down further into the techniques, you wouldn't go into a baseball "batting cage" to train on that skill with someone who is a "mindset coach" or "life coach" or "executive coach" who has never swung a bat (much less possesses the expert level proficiency of doing the technique perfectly).

Imagine a martial arts or baseball coach who only talked to you about mindset and asked you a lot of reflection questions but didn't teach you how to correctly practice your new techniques, or worse, didn't even know the techniques in the first place?

Kind of obvious when you think about it, right?

Repetition is the mother of skill. So, I will repeat this crucial point.

> *The only effective way to learn technical and complex skills (baseball, basketball, playing a musical instrument, martial arts, flying an airplane or leadership) is to break the ability down into its component parts or "skill sets" and then train, memorize and internalize each of those techniques until they become second nature.*

Learning complex skills follows a pattern that looks like this. Again, you already know this because you have already mastered numerous complex skills. So let me remind you what you already know.

Over many weeks, practices become habits. Over many months, habits become skills. With time and ongoing practice, those skills combine into "skill sets." Ultimately, the skill sets come together to form the "ability" (the complex skill) that the learner is practicing.

To be competent at baseball, an athlete must have the skills to throw, catch, hit and run. To be competent at MMA, an athlete must have wrestling, kickboxing, and grappling skills.

For the past 20+ years, all of my leadership trainings have used "Deliberate Practice" principles from "Expert Performance Theory." This is central to why my leadership trainings consistently produce results where most leadership training programs fail.

Two decades ago, I was the first to apply *Expert Performance Theory* and *Deliberate Practice* to leadership development at Integral Institute (where I was a senior faculty member) and the Stagen Leadership Academy (that I co-founded) when I created the original "Integral Leadership Program." That program is still running 22 years later (and still going strong).

As pioneers in this practice-based approach to leadership development, is safe to say that my partners and I have more experience than anyone else in the world with it.

We literally invented the category of "practice-based leadership."

I have personally spent 20 hours a week, 50 weeks a year for over 20 years training, mentoring, and coaching leaders, totaling around 1,000 hours per year. The "10,000 hour rule," popularized by Malcolm Gladwell's book "Outliers," suggests that it takes about 10,000 hours for someone to become an expert or master a complex skill such as medicine, martial arts, management, or leadership. I have logged more than 10,000 hours *training leaders* and additional 10,000 hours *coaching leaders*, for a total of over 20,000 hours. This provides me with a breadth of relevant experience and depth of understanding of leadership development that very few people have.

I am not telling you this to impress you. I am telling you this to impress upon you that the information in this book is coming from someone who has vast experience using these methods and who is a legitimate "expert" as defined by Expert Performance Theory. I am telling you this in the hopes of motivating and inspiring you to adopt these methods and use them in your own leadership development and in your organization.

These methods work, and they work better than most of the other leadership development methods you are likely to encounter.

All of this experience has led me to one crucial conclusion: *the only effective way to learn the complex skill we call leadership is to use a technique- and practice-based approach.*

This insight and this belief flies in the face of convention.

Approximately 80-90% of the leadership training programs on the market focus on character traits, abstract "qualities" of leaders, and vague concepts like "EQ" yet offer no specific techniques or skills to practice to develop emotional intelligence. (More on EQ later.)

The straight truth is this: To learn complex skills, especially leadership, you need training on individual techniques and then you must practice those techniques until they become internalized, and then over time, combine those growing skills together to form new abilities.

The phrase "10,000 hours" is likely familiar to many readers, but few know its origins. It was popularized by Malcom Gladwell in his book *Outliers: The Story of Success,* but the term was originally coined by Anders Ericsson, who researched and developed the method called "Deliberate Practice." Ericsson's research showed that only certain types of practice lead to high-performance or expert-level skills, not all practice.

When you leverage this method called "deliberate practice" in our management and leadership skill learning efforts, you can expect to dramatically increase the rate at which you can level up abilities. And while it could take 5-10 years to achieve that 10,000 hour "expert" level performance in leadership skills, we can expect massive gains in performance in just half a year to a year if you follow the guidelines that "expert performance theory" and this book explain.

My experience shows that following my Accelerating Leadership method (which in my programs includes micro learning tutorial videos and weekly group coaching on Zoom), a leader can go from beginner to intermediate, or intermediate to expert in only about 6-12 months. If you apply all the things you are learning in this book series (all four books), even without the benefit of my micro-learning tutorial videos and my group coaching on Zoom, you could still go from beginner to intermediate or intermediate to expert level in just a couple of years.

There is an old saying that goes, "Practice makes perfect".

Like so many old sayings, this one points to something true and useful, but isn't really accurate. Sure, practice is important and certainly helpful. But if you are practicing in any way other than the perfect "form" then that is actually reinforcing wrong technique.

Learning the wrong form of a technique is hardly what any reasonable person would call "makes perfect".

So, we can correct that misconception by restating it this way... *Perfect practice makes perfect.*

This idea of "perfect practice" is not just a figure of speech. Nor does it point merely to the correct form of a technique mentioned previously. "Perfect practice" is about a very specific type of practice that dramatically accelerates learning and crushes the steep learning curves associated with complex skills.

While this relatively new kind of "practice" is starting to gain popularity, most people have either never heard of it, or have perhaps heard of it but don't know how to engage it and use it.

As mentioned prior, the person who pioneered much of the research in this area and coined the term "Deliberate Practice" was Anders Ericsson. He has written several books, but I will highlight two here.

They are: *The Cambridge Handbook of Expertise and Expert Performance* and *Peak: Secrets from the New Science of Expertise.*

Ericsson's research suggests that only certain types of practice can lead to expertise. George Leonard also described a similar concept in his book: *Mastery: The Keys to Success and Long-Term Fulfillment.* I will use Anders Ericsson's own words to define and clarify exactly what deliberate practice is...

> *"Deliberate practice develops skills that other people have already figured out how to do and for which effective training techniques have been established. The practice regimen should be designed and overseen by a teacher or coach who is familiar with the abilities of expert performers and with how those abilities can best be developed."*

Ericsson found that surgeons, for example, use deliberate practice, which involves specific goals and immediate feedback. Surgeons can see how their actions impact their patient's health and make improvements quickly.

Radiologists, on the other hand, don't have the same connection between their diagnosis and the outcome (the long-term health of their patients). While this example highlights the critical importance of specific goals and feedback, Ericsson strongly emphasizes that it's not enough to merely mirror the behaviors of the experts.

It's important to understand the thinking, the reasoning and the feelings behind those behaviors. In plain terms, it's not enough to just parrot behaviors that would be how the behavior looks from the outside. You must also understand how that technique feels from the inside. What does the expert, the exemplar, think and feel when they are performing the technique?

Ericsson's research showed that the quality of these internal representations separates experts from novices. This applies to every field they have studied, including rock climbing, music, sports, research, writing, memory skills, and sales.

It's important to note that you cannot create optimal "internal representations" (how the technique is experienced from the inside) just by doing an activity over and over again. Rather, you need to model the internal representations of an exemplar who has the skill you want to acquire. This is why I will frequently remind you throughout this book that the fastest way to learn leadership skills is to get mentoring, guidance and coaching from people who are experts in those specific techniques.

To truly understand a skill, it's not enough to just hear about it or read about it, you must experience it and practice it over and over until it becomes habit. This is one of the main reasons that most leadership development programs fail to develop leader. They usually teach the wrong things in the wrong way. If they aren't teaching specific skills then they aren't actually helping people get better at the technical and complex skill called leadership.

To progress in your leadership skills, your facilitators and coaches must be experts in both the techniques they are teaching and the best methods to teach those techniques. If their "leadership model" does not emphasize specific techniques and practices, and if their advice to help leaders get better at the technical and complex skill of leadership does not incorporate "deliberate practice," then I strongly suggest you look elsewhere.

Further, if your leadership trainer or coach is not a "black belt" (an expert) in the techniques they are coaching you in, then they are not qualified to coach you.

You must get this.

> *If you spend money on leadership coaches who are not experts in the specific skills of leadership, then you are wasting your time and your money. And this includes the ubiquitous "mindset coaches" who will happily take your money but can't teach you anything about leadership. People who say "mindset is everything" don't know much about anything. Mindset is most definitely not everything. Its not even the main thing. Mindset is 20% at most. Strategy and technique is 80% or more of what leads to success in any endeavor.*

Mindset coaching is mainly helpful for people <u>who already know how to do a technique perfectly</u> and they are trying to adopt the best psychology (mindset) to help them do it more consistently. Mindset coaching is great for professional athletes who are already at the very top of their game and who know the techniques well.

Executive coaches and self-described leadership coaches who focus primarily on mindset, in my experience, do this because the do not know the strategies, skills or techniques of leadership.

In my opinion, if they did know the techniques of leadership, they would be sharing them with their clients (a lot more than mindset). To be blunt, focusing on mindset is a primary way that unqualified leadership coaches cover up their lack of knowledge about leadership. Do them a favor and share this book with them. Maybe they will choose to level up their knowledge about leadership.

As mentioned earlier in this book, leadership advice-givers can't agree on a single definition of effective leadership because they have different worldviews and as such, see different approaches (or styles) of leadership as more appealing (based on the values, assumptions and beliefs inherent in their specific worldview). I spent over a decade working with Ken Wilber at Integral Institute and my R&D team at Stagen Leadership Academy, and more than a million of dollars developing and testing the "Unifying Theory of Leadership" that provides the theoretical foundation for this work.

This book summarizes the resulting breakthroughs in understanding leadership, instructional design for leadership training programs, and strategies for rapidly raising effective leadership skills. This book discloses this well-kept trade secret, which we've used for nearly two decades to train over 10,000 corporate executives (and many leaders in developing countries through my nonprofit organization).

I hope you can appreciate the value of the research, frameworks, models and tools that you now hold in your hands. I have spent well over a million dollars of my own money, and many millions of dollars of my company's money over a twenty-year period in order to now be in a position to bring you the "simplicity on the other side of complexity" reflected in this model.

I spent five years working with Ken Wilber and Integral Institute to create the original *Unifying Theory of Leadership*. I spent ten additional years testing the model with corporate leaders, simplifying and refining it, resulting in my *Leadership Rosetta Stone*. Then I spent another five years expanding the testing beyond the corporate world to also include international humanitarian efforts, governments, military leaders, religious and even tribal and indigenous leaders in third-world countries, culminating in the *Universal Leadership Model* presented in this book (and my other books).

I tell you this not to impress you; rather, to impress upon you the real value contained in this book that you now own, and hopefully to inspire you to learn, internalize, and most importantly, put into practice these extremely valuable academically-sound, time-tested methods.

In this book, I provide a sufficient overview of the practice-based approach for you to apply in your leadership development efforts (in the Strategy & Alignment dimension of leadership).

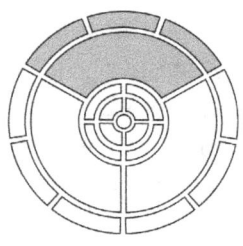

CHAPTER 5: BENCHMARKING THE STRATEGY & ALIGNMENT LEADERSHIP CAPACITY

In the "Integral Leadership Framework" presented previously, I briefly introduced you to this area of responsibility that all leaders share. In this next part of the book, we will take a deeper dive into this dimension and unpack these three essential skill sets leaders use to fulfill these responsibilities. First, in this short chapter, I will provide you benchmarks for this "overall dimension" of leadership that I call Strategy & Alignment These benchmarks are "high level" for the whole "essential ability" as I also call this dimension. Recall that there are three dimensions of leadership. These were all three summarized previously and I have published one book per dimension. Before we move on to subsequent chapters, where we drill down into each "skill set" in this dimension, it is important to establish benchmarks for this overall "capacity" for Strategy & Alignment. Also, you will find that in subsequent chapters (one per skill set), I will also provide benchmarks for each of the discrete "skill sets" that leaders utilize in this dimension. Those benchmarks will be more granular (per skill set) as contrasted with this high-level view of a leader's proficiency in the overall "essential ability" we refer to as Strategy & Stakeholders. Consider assessing how you "measure up" against these established benchmarks. Keep in mind that, statistically speaking, most people tend to fall within the middle range of a typical "bell curve". Therefore, most readers of this book will likely fall somewhere in the "intermediate" range of proficiency in this essential ability, the dimension of leadership. If you were to fall in the lower range, then you have some immediate work to do to avoid undermining your leadership credibility.

My hope is that, after reading this book, adopting the best practices outlined here, and engaging in these activities in your leadership role with your team for several months, you will begin to see your proficiency level improve from "intermediate" to "late intermediate." And with a few more months of practice, I hope that you will progress into the "early advanced" level of proficiency.

Over time, if you socialize these practices with your team, it is possible to get your whole team to reach the "advanced" (or "higher levels") of proficiency in this essential ability that I am calling Strategy & Alignment.

Once you move into the next chapters on the more granular specific skill sets, it is more likely that you will find one in which you (or members of your team or certain teams) fall into the lower range. But let's not get ahead of ourselves. Let's take a moment and get grounded in this essential leadership ability called Strategy & Alignment. (Recall that earlier I also called these three dimensions the "Inherent Leadership Responsibilities." So let's take an honest look at how your leadership measures up in this essential leadership ability and this inherent responsibility.

Definition

First let's define. The essential leadership ability that I am calling "Strategy & Alignment includes all of the activities related to establishing and communicating the purpose, vision, and values of the organization, making sense of what is happening in the current environment including evaluating relevant challenges and opportunities, strategic thinking, prioritizing strategic objectives, crafting strategic plans, and enrolling stakeholder commitment in the organizational vision and the strategy to achieve shared goals. It is helpful to orient our thinking about this dimension of leadership by reviewing some of the key questions, challenges and goals that leaders have when addressing this area of leadership.

Figuring Out the Big Picture and Setting the Right Direction

Great leadership begins with clarity of direction. Planning is the ability to analyze complex situations, anticipate challenges, and set clear priorities so that teams and organizations move forward with focus and purpose. Leaders who excel in planning don't just react to daily problems—they proactively chart the path ahead, ensuring that all efforts align with long-term goals.

A leader without strong planning skills will find their teams constantly putting out fires, working on low-impact tasks, or heading in different directions. Without clear priorities, employees waste time on projects that don't contribute to business success, and teams struggle to adapt when circumstances change. Planning prevents confusion and misalignment by providing a structured approach to decision-making and problem-solving.

Planning is more than just setting goals—it's about knowing where to focus effort, how to allocate resources, and when to adjust strategies. A senior manager with strong planning skills gathers information from multiple sources, identifies key trends, and connects the dots between different challenges. They don't make decisions based on gut instinct alone; instead, they use data, insights, and discussions with stakeholders to ensure that their plans are well-informed and adaptable.

For example, imagine a senior manager in a healthcare company overseeing multiple hospital units. Without strong planning, each department might operate independently, making decisions that conflict with overall hospital priorities. But with effective planning, the leader ensures that staffing, budgets, and patient care initiatives are all aligned, preventing inefficiencies and ensuring high-quality service.

Planning also includes organizational steering, which means that leaders regularly review progress, reassess priorities, and adjust plans as needed. The best leaders recognize that no plan is perfect, and they create systems that allow their teams to pivot when necessary without losing momentum.

A lack of effective planning and direction setting creates chaos, inefficiency, and frustration, but strong planning leads to clarity, alignment, and smart decision-making. Leaders who develop this ability set their teams up for success by ensuring that every action contributes to a larger, well-thought-out strategy.

It is helpful to orient our thinking about this crucial dimension of leadership by reviewing some of the key questions, challenges, and goals that leaders have when addressing this area of leadership.

Strategic Clarity and Prioritized Focus

At the senior level, leadership is not about reacting to tasks or maintaining momentum—it's about thinking clearly, setting direction, and aligning energy and resources with what matters most. The Planning dimension reflects this core leadership responsibility: to define strategy, interpret complexity, and ensure that individuals, teams, and departments are focused on high-leverage objectives that support the organization's mission.

Strategy & Alignment is not the same as being "visionary." Nor is it about having a personal instinct for strategy. This dimension is a trainable leadership ability—one that consists of three concrete skill sets: Sensemaking, Stakeholder Alignment, and Organizational Steering. Together, they allow senior leaders to generate clarity, focus, and commitment across the system.

When this dimension is underdeveloped, teams drift. Energy is wasted on low-priority initiatives. Leaders get stuck treating symptoms instead of identifying root causes. Teams work hard, but outcomes stall. Without strong Planning skills, even high-performing organizations lose traction—not because they aren't executing, but because they're executing on the wrong things.
On the other hand, when senior leaders operate at a high level in the Planning dimension, three core outcomes emerge:

1. Strategic Clarity: Everyone understands what matters most and why.
2. Prioritized Focus: Resources and attention are directed toward the most important work.
3. Shared Commitment: Teams and stakeholders support the direction because they see how their efforts connect to the whole.

Senior leaders who are strong in Planning don't just talk about vision—they translate complexity into clarity. They apply structured thinking to complex challenges, communicate strategic intent in ways others can act on, and make disciplined trade-offs between what's important and what's merely urgent. This dimension is the foundation of all leadership impact. Without it, leaders are guessing. With it, they lead with strong direction and smart planning.

Strategy & Alignment Questions

Following are some of the common questions leaders ask about this essential ability:

• What is the best way to make sense out of our organizational landscape so that we can identify the best solutions for our challenges and opportunities?

• What is the best way to clarify our organization's vision and mission and engage all of our key stakeholders for maximum alignment and commitment?

• How should we develop our organizational goals, strategies and plans, prioritize the highest-leverage projects and communicate them to our teams effectively?

Strategy & Alignment Challenges

Following are some of the common challenges leaders report about this essential ability:

• Inadequate or weak sensemaking (analysis) leading to weak business strategies or bad decisions

• Need for the organization to pivot (but there is inertia and inadequate cooperation to make the shift)

• Stakeholders are not aligned and not bought in, stakeholder incentives are misaligned or in conflict

• Uncertainty (and fear) about the future, lack of agreement about what the organization should do

• Rapidly changing environment, uncertain environment (VUCA: volatility, uncertainty, complexity, ambiguity)

- The annual planning cycle is too slow, rigid, inefficient and outdated within a quarter or two

- Strategic planning tied to a budget rather than strategic organizational priorities

- The need to re-organize (execute a re-org) but there are numerous obstacles to overcome

Strategy & Alignment Goals

Following are some of the common goals leaders have regarding this essential ability:

- Do a better job of shared sensemaking, working together to analyze challenges (and opportunities)

- Increase ability to understand what is really happening and what is needed

- Find ways to strengthen strategic thinking skills for leaders, managers and teams

- More leverage, more focus, better at prioritizing opportunities, objectives, initiatives and projects

- Elevate team (organization's) strategic planning tools, skills and methods (better plans, more buy in)

- Align/enroll stakeholders with organization's vision and strategy (for greater commitment and cooperation)

Precision Proficiency Benchmarking

A leader's skill proficiency in any of these dimensions is determined less by looking at the leader, a better gauge of the leader's proficiency is to look at the results observed in the organization. Therefore, on the following pages you will find the benchmarks to use when evaluating a leader and their team or organization's current capability in this dimension. These organizational benchmarks are very helpful to use when asking members of a team to self-assess the team's current capabilities. Not only does this provide valuable insights to the leaders, but it also is a terrific conversation starter that you can use to discuss this aspect of the team's (or department or organization's) strengths and gaps which could be elevated to support the group's ability to achieve its shared objectives.

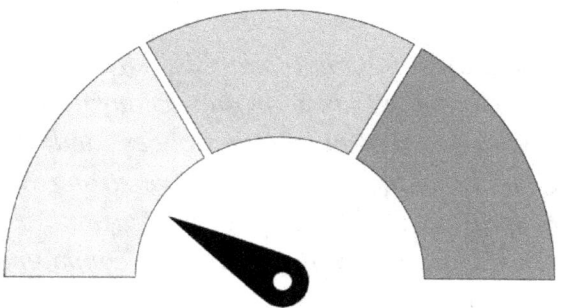

STRATEGY & ALIGNMENT LOWER RANGE

At this low level of proficiency, leaders struggle to bring clarity or structure to their team's priorities. Strategic direction is vague, reactive, or overly generic because leaders have weak strategic thinking and planning skills. Efforts are often scattered across too many initiatives. There is little distinction between what is important and what is simply urgent. Stakeholder engagement tends to be low because the rationale behind decisions is unclear. Teams experience friction, confusion, and rework as a result.

- Strategic plans, if they exist, are shallow, under-communicated, or outdated
- Organizational energy is spread thin across misaligned or low-leverage tasks.
- Little or no root cause analysis is performed before making decisions.
- Stakeholders lack clarity or buy-in around vision, values, and goals.

Leader Self-Description:

I wouldn't say that situational analysis, strategic thinking or stakeholder commitment is strong in our organization. We rely on our gut to evaluate current circumstances and decide what strategies we should deploy. We don't have strong written plans for the year or quarter. Our "organizational vision" is not clearly articulated. The level of cooperation and commitment of our stakeholders is on the lower side.

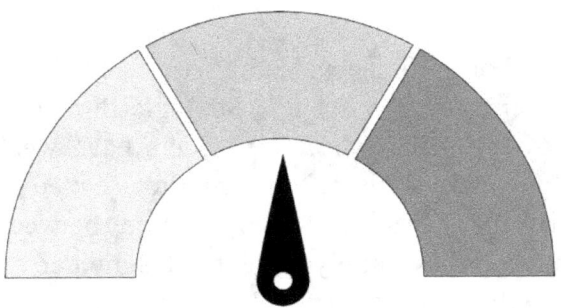

STRATEGY & ALIGNMENT INTERMEDIATE RANGE

At this level of proficiency, Leaders begin to engage in planning conversations and make efforts to understand what matters most. They produce strategic plans and articulate some goals, but execution is still fragmented due to inconsistent prioritization or vague alignment. While stakeholders may be included, the messaging and rationale are not always clear or compelling. Strategic traction improves in some areas, but performance varies across functions.

- Strategic plans are created but lack cross-functional integration or follow-through.

- Priorities are identified but shift too often or compete with one another.

- Some effort is made to align stakeholders, but commitment varies.
- Root cause thinking is used occasionally, but not as a regular discipline.

Leader Self-Description:

We do put some effort into trying to understand the "core drivers" impacting us before we attempt to craft a strategy and make plans. We have written annual and quarterly plans. We have articulated our organizational vision statement (or mission). We need to do a better job of enrolling our stakeholders and getting their buy-in and commitment.

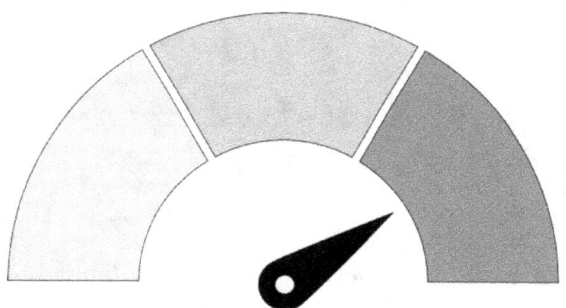

STRATEGY & ALIGNMENT HIGHER RANGE

At this high range of proficiency, leaders consistently demonstrate strategic thinking and use disciplined planning craft high-leverage strategies and tactics. They define clear priorities and communicate them in ways that connect to vision and values. Stakeholders across the organization understand not just what to do, but why it matters. Strategic plans are dynamic, data-informed, and adaptable without being reactive. Resources are allocated based on impact, not noise. The result is focused energy, alignment, and measurable momentum.

- Strategic plans are grounded in analysis, clearly communicated, and reviewed regularly.
- Priorities are few, focused, and tightly aligned to long-term strategy.
- Stakeholders understand the "why" behind goals and commit to shared direction.
- Root cause clarity and leverage thinking guide decision-making and resource allocation.

Leader Self-Description:

Our organization is great at "vision," "strategic thinking and planning" and achieving "shared stakeholder commitment." Some of our leaders brought in tools that help us discern key drivers and root causes to use to craft high-leverage strategies. Our annual initiatives and quarterly objectives are dynamically linked to ongoing projects. We have well-articulated vision / mission / values statements and enjoy high levels of stakeholder commitment.

Now that you have grounded in the levels of proficiency (low, intermediate and high) in this overall dimension, we will move into the subsequent chapters, one per skill set, and we will review the benchmarks for those specific skill sets and many of the most important and most helpful skills, techniques, tools and practices that bolster a leaders ability in each of these skill sets. The first skill set is "Sensemaking."

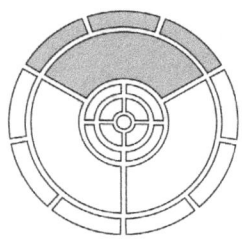

CHAPTER 6: SENSEMAKING

First we begin with a clear definition and the benchmarks for levels of proficiency in this skill set. This skill set is concerned with your ability to evaluate the landscape (both external conditions as well as internal organizational dynamics) to determine what is really happening, the key drivers impacting the environment, what is most important for your organization, and what is most needed.

Team Discussion

When you initiate a conversation with your employees and team(s), you could use some version of the following questions.

• How do we currently evaluate the landscape our organization is operating in?

• How do we identify the external conditions as well as internal organizational dynamics?

• How do we determine what is really happening, what key drivers are impacting the environment, and what is most important and needed for our team / department / organization?

Benchmarks

Next, we move into the benchmarks for this skill set.

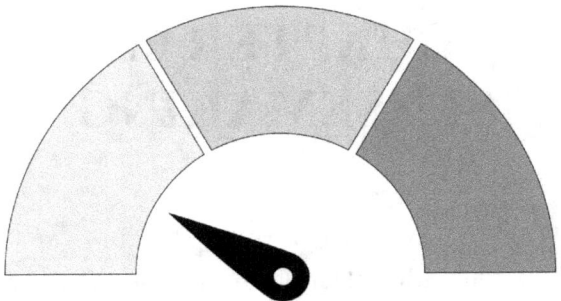

SENSEMAKING LOWER RANGE

A leader and a team functioning in the lower range of proficiency in this skill set might describe it this way.

We usually move into action quickly after a quick assessment of circumstances using our best judgment, however, we do not have specific training or use any kind of sophisticated tools to evaluate or investigate complex situations and circumstances.

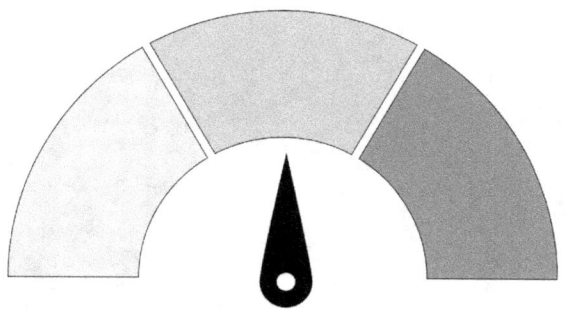

SENSEMAKING INTERMEDIATE RANGE

A leader and a team functioning in the middle range of proficiency in this skill set might describe it this way.

My team and I discuss circumstances together and try to understand the core drivers impacting our situation before we decide on the best course of action. Beyond a discussion, we don't utilize specific sense-making frameworks or any kind of sophisticated investigative tools.

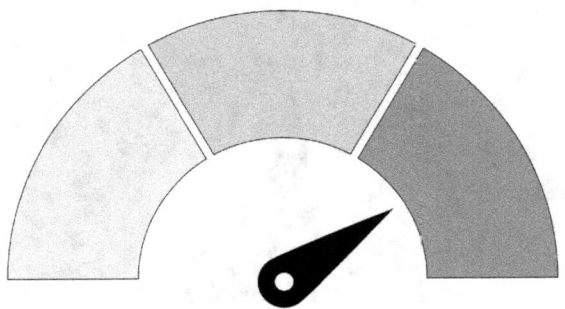

SENSEMAKING HIGHER RANGE

A leader and a team functioning in the higher range of proficiency in this skill set might describe it this way.

My team and I use one or more analytical tools to investigate situations. We always try to take multiple perspectives into account during our discussion, and in most cases, we are gaining visibility into the key drivers and root causes of situations before we build a solution or decide on a strategy.

Sensemaking Primer

> *All of the great leaders have had one characteristic in common: it was the willingness to confront unequivocally the major anxiety of their people in their time. This, and not much else, is the essence of leadership.*
> *— John Kenneth Galbraith*

We will start this section by asking you to reflect for a moment, in your own experience, what makes leaders successful in their leadership role?

As a leader, it's important to be aware of what's happening in your environment and make informed decisions that benefit those who report to you. Remember, a lot is riding on your shoulders. So, it's crucial to stay focused, make good judgments, and have sound reasoning when it comes to your actions and decisions. For leaders to be successful and effective over time, they need to bring awareness, intelligence, and judgment to every situation.

Good leadership involves being aware of your surroundings and using your intelligence and judgment to make informed decisions. The best leaders also have a team of knowledgeable, experienced people who help them observe and interpret situations and determine what's needed.

More than five decades ago, organizational psychologist Karl Weick introduced a term for this process.

While this is not a term familiar to all leaders yet, it is an important concept and even more important skill that leaders are already using, whether they have heard of the term or not. The term is sensemaking.

Central to the very idea of leadership is that the leader is moving, with the organization, over time, toward a shared vision.

To stay on track, it's important to have a clear understanding of the "territory" you're operating in. This concept, called a "map of the territory," becomes even more important as you improve your ability to make sense of your circumstances.

Fundamental to the concept of leadership effectiveness are three sensemaking activities.

First, leadership must understand what's going on in the environment in which the organization is operating.

It is essential that leadership has an adequately comprehensive and at least marginally accurate understanding of the essential question "What is happening?"

Second, leadership must create a map or "mental model" of the environment with an emphasis on the changes that have recently occurred or are currently occurring.

It is crucial that the leader does this both "with others" and also "for others" so that there is a shared understanding of the changes occurring in the environment and what these changes mean for the organization.

Third, leadership must continually revise this "map" as "the territory" changes over time.

As a leader, it's important to constantly update your understanding of the environment and make sure you're using an accurate and up-to-date map to guide your decision-making. If you don't, you're not fulfilling one of your most fundamental responsibilities. Think about it like this: a map helps you navigate, and a good map is accurate and up-to-date. Is your map of the world (your understanding of what's happening in your organization) complete, comprehensive, and accurate? Or are you trying to lead with a map that's incomplete, inaccurate, or outdated?

Maps of current (and changing) conditions, and "mental models" are the topics of much research in the fields of organizational development, organizational psychology, integral psychology, and developmental psychology.

In this section, we will draw some important distinctions between three essential different terms: *Sensemaking, Meaning Making* and *Mental Models*.

As you progress in your leadership effectiveness, and as you mature in your role as leader, these three concepts will become essential "go-to tools" in your expanding leadership toolkit.

Much has been written about all three of these crucial leadership concepts. Let us differentiate Sensemaking from the related terms *Meaning Making and Mental Models*.

As mentioned previously, sensemaking is a term that was originally coined in the 1970s by organizational psychologist Karl Weick. He defined sensemaking as "the process by which people give meaning to their collective experiences."

This term Sensemaking, and the practice that it points to, has been popularized more recently by MIT Sloan School of Management professor of organizational studies and leadership, Deborah Ancona. She describes sensemaking as, "Being able to make sense of the world and understand the context your organization is operating in."

Ancona summarizes this crucial leadership practice as...

"Getting out to see what is going on in the environment, creating a mental model or map of that environment with and for other people in the organization, and then revising that map or model as things change."

Ancona helps managers understand what's going on in their environment by creating a map, testing it with others, and refining or abandoning it based on its credibility. This skill, called sensemaking, helps leaders make better decisions and drive progress and growth in their organization

Meaning Making

Weick was an organizational psychologist, as such, when he used the term "Sensemaking," he was specifically referring to what we might call "Shared Sensemaking" or "Organizational Sensemaking".

We can contrast this group emphasis with the term "Meaning Making" which is a central concept in developmental psychology and constructivist learning theory (also known as "Educational Psychology").

As used by psychologists, the term Meaning Making is defined as "the process of how people construe, understand, or make sense of life events, relationships, and the self."

In this book, we use a kind of shorthand when we say Meaning Making is "how people construct their views of self, others and system."

In a still broader sense, Meaning Making is the primary research object of semiotics and semantics, or put more simply, "the study of signs and symbols and their use or interpretation."

Developmental psychology, popularized by Robert Kegan and Ken Wilber, is the study of how people grow and change over time. You may have heard of Jean Piaget, the founder of this field, and his famous "stages of cognitive development" that we can see in children and young adults. This field is more focused on how individuals construct their own meaning, rather than shared meaning within a group. This is important for leadership because it helps leaders understand how their team members make sense of things. In fact, not considering this can lead to ineffective leadership and failed leadership training programs.

Meaning making is central to how individuals and organizations define and interpret the interpersonal phenomenon we call "leadership."

As we will learn in other sections of this book, different people use different meaning making mechanisms to construct very different "worldviews".

People's beliefs and trust in leadership are largely influenced by their diverse worldviews and "meaning making systems," which help them understand and make sense of the world. As a leader, it's important to consider the different perspectives of those you lead and the community you serve.

Mental Models

Organizational psychologists define mental models as "an explanation of someone's thought process about how something works in the real world".

It is helpful to differentiate Mental Models from worldviews. A person's worldview is their overarching "view of self, others and system"

The term Mental Model refers to a person's internal map of some smaller, more specific part of their world, we could say, it is a person's internal cognitive model of "how something works," or stated more precisely, "how this person thinks something works".

As far back as 1943, Scottish psychologist Kenneth Craik suggested that the mind constructs "small-scale models of reality that it uses to anticipate events".

Mental models are personal beliefs about how things work that shape our thoughts, actions, and perceptions. They help us understand and solve problems. You can think of them as personal algorithms for tackling tasks. Essentially, mental models are internal representations of external reality that influence our cognition, decision-making, and behavior.

Mental models are largely composed of embedded assumptions, generalizations and even images. Our numerous models aggregate to shape our overall worldview and, in turn, impact how we perceive reality, and how we respond to those perceptions with behavior.

Sometimes, two people can see the same thing but have different understandings of it because of their own experiences and beliefs. People often describe events based on their own perspectives, which can be influenced by their mental models (even if they don't realize it).

In a very real sense, mental models are like the corrective lenses in eyeglasses. They significantly change our perception of whatever it is we are looking at. And like the corrective lenses in eyeglasses, most people forget about (or are unaware) of these lenses that are changing or distorting their perception.

"Organizational Learning" pioneer Peter Senge popularized the term Mental Models for mainstream business and other modern institutions in his bestselling books *The Fifth Discipline: The Art & Practice of The Learning Organization and The Fifth Discipline Fieldbook: Strategies and Tools for Building a Learning Organization.*

Prior to that, Harvard management school professor and pioneer in the fields of management consulting and organizational psychology, Chris Argyris developed what he called a "Ladder of Inference" to describe how people form and sustain these mental models.

Argyris and his colleagues and students showed business managers how they all make assumptions in their daily lives and how they can better work with their own and others' assumptions and interpretations.
As we will explain in another section of this book, assumptions are a necessary and useful part of our mental models.

The important leadership practice that we call "Working with Assumptions and Interpretations" will be explored in another section of this book.

Understanding Sensemaking as a Leadership Skill Set

Sensemaking refers to how leaders structure the unknown so that they can "make sense" of what is happening and respond accordingly in ways that support steering their organization toward shared outcomes and goals.

A leader engages the practice of sensemaking so that they can construct a plausible and pragmatic understanding of the shifting environment their organization is operating in.

"Sensemaking" may be a new term to some, but it's something we all do constantly. It's the process of understanding our experiences and making decisions based on them. All leaders, throughout history, have used sensemaking to guide their actions, even if they didn't have access to advanced tools. In today's uncertain world, it's more important than ever for leaders to be skilled at sensemaking, because if they're not, they risk leading their organizations astray.

An institution's stakeholders rely on its leaders to recognize and interpret patterns in the complexity of technology innovations, external signals including frequently-changing community landscape, political shifts, a constantly changing media and communication landscape, and cultural changes inside and outside of the organization.

Leaders must ask themselves…

>   What is really happening?

>   What is needed?

>   Do our previous actions still make sense now?

>   Would it make more sense to change what we are doing?

In this section, we drew important distinctions between sensemaking, meaning making and mental models. Being a good leader means having a strong set of tools to help guide your team. In this book, we'll go into more detail on specific techniques and practices you can use to improve your sensemaking skills. The better you are at sensemaking, the better you'll be able to lead your organization towards shared goals and vision. In the next sections we will look more closely at sensemaking principles.

Sensemaking Principles

Organizational psychologist Karl Weick, who coined the term, identified seven principles of Sensemaking that can inform how we engage this essential leadership practice with our teams and in our organizations.

1. Sensemaking is an Extension of Identity

Weick was one of the first researchers to recognize that a person's sense of identity and what and who they "identify with" plays a central role in how they "make sense" of their experiences.

Put another way, who people think they are in a given context (such as a team or department) shapes how they interpret events and how they respond to those interpretations about events.

2. Sensemaking is Largely Retrospective

Reflecting on past events provides people with a crucial opportunity for Sensemaking. The more that people engage in retrospection, or reflection as it is sometimes called, the more nuanced their Sensemaking becomes.

When people and organizations don't make the time, or are prevented by their environment from engaging adequate reflection and introspection, their Sensemaking will be negatively impacted and their resulting Mental Models will be partial, inaccurate or even fundamentally flawed.

Naturally this then impacts their problem solving, their approaches, and ultimately their decision making.

3. Sensemaking Emerges from Narrative

Human beings use narratives to organize their experiences.

Narratives are in simple terms the stories they tell ourselves and the stories that emerge in dialog with others.

Humans use language as a primary way to make sense of their experiences. Dialogue is very important for Sensemaking both for individuals and groups. As people speak and dialogue with each other, they construct narrative accounts of what they think has happened and what they think is
happening.

Articulating their thoughts helps them understand what they think and helps them organize their past experiences and also helps them more accurately anticipate future events.

We will explore narratives and the "stories" we tell ourselves more deeply in another section in this book.

4. Sensemaking is Social

As mentioned before, Sensemaking, as described by Weick and other organizational psychologists, is largely a social activity. It can be viewed as an interpersonal phenomenon.

As members of a group share their individual Sensemaking threads, they weave a collective tapestry of shared meaning.

In a group, certain ideas are often emphasized and repeated, while others may be challenged or dismissed. This process is not typically guided by scientific method or accuracy. However, wise leaders can shape these conversations to ensure that the shared understanding of the group is more grounded in reality or at least more helpful, rather than just reflecting people's biases and misunderstandings.

Unfortunately, dialogue skills are not equally distributed across the leadership population. In fact, some leaders have never actually learned to dialogue, and in the worst cases, to even listen. We will explore these important topics in the Conscious Communication section of this book.

5. Sensemaking is Continuous

As individuals and groups react to the environments they face, they simultaneously shape their environments (whether they are consciously aware of this dynamic or not).

As people interact with their environment, they observe the consequences of their actions on it. This creates a feedback loop that gives people an opportunity to learn about how accurate their interpretations are and informs their sense of identity in their context.

Over time, this ongoing feedback process shapes their sense of identity in the group and in their context based on how others behave toward them.

This then, in turn, influences how they behave in an attempt to influence others and how others see and relate to them. This is central to teamwork dynamics and how culture is created and influenced. We will be exploring this in more detail when we drill into the Creating the Container skill set (In my other book on *Teamwork & Culture*)

6. Context Offers Clues

All meaning is context-dependent. Put another way, what something means is largely a function of the context, or the environment, in which the object or action occurs.

While some people pay little conscious attention to context, it nevertheless shapes their Sensemaking. Different contexts render different things less important, more important, helpful or harmful.

It's not that much of an overstatement to say, "Context is everything." It certainly has everything to do with what things mean. A given context helps people decide what information is relevant and what explanations are plausible, useful, appealing, acceptable or not acceptable.

And it goes without saying that every context is unique which imbues the same fact or action with different meaning depending on the context it occurs in. This principle was introduced as "Context Offers Clues." Stated in slightly more technical terms, we might say that "cues" we extract from context offers us "clues" that can help us connect the dots between different points of reference that link specific ideas to broader networks of meaning.

7. Plausibility is Preferred Over Accuracy

As mentioned previously, individual meaning making and collective sensemaking is happening continuously and is not generally constrained by

accuracy. Whether a person or groups' Sensemaking is accurate, much less scientific, is beside the point.

Human meaning making and group sensemaking consists of countless data points, assumptions about that data, and different interpretations of events based on largely unconscious, unexamined and/or untested assumptions.

Accuracy, comprehensiveness, and usefulness are important to many people, but Weick found that groups usually prefer a plausible answer to a complex question over a complex but accurate one. You can see this happening in the news, social media, and other parts of popular culture, where simple but wrong answers are often accepted as truth, even if people have been exposed to the correct but more complex answers.

This is another example that shows us how incredibly essential it is that leaders bring as much wisdom and discernment that they can muster to influence the "ongoing conversation" and be vigilant with a "hand on the rudder" to influence the ever-present Sensemaking activities their organization is engaging in.

Deborah Ancona and Sensemaking

Deborah Ancona, from MIT Sloan School of Management, expanded on this concept as part of her "X-Teams" model, which posits that effective teams need to work both internally and externally. In her framework, she identified four key leadership capabilities: *Sensemaking, Relating, Visioning, and Inventing.*

In her view, sensemaking is so important, that it is one of four pillars of her leadership model (along with relating, visioning and inventing).

She defines sensemaking as, the the process of gathering data, seeking patterns, and creating a map of the competitive landscape. She sees sensemaking as the foundation of her four-part leadership model since a clear understanding of the external environment is the critical starting point before setting a vision or implementing other strategies (including what she calls "inventing).

Ancona, and many other business and leadership professors acknowledge the leaders critical role in guiding the organization's sensemaking process, especially during times of change. Today's business environment for many if not most companies is characterized by constant change.

From Ancona's perspective, leaders are responsible for sensemaking in the following ways:

1. Leaders help frame the issue or event.

2. They influence which cues or signals are deemed important.

3. Leaders set the narrative, determining the story told about the event or situation.

4. Leadership facilitate a collective understanding, helping to unify teams or organizations.

Five Sensemaking Implementation Practices

It is important to understand that sensemaking is first and foremost a leadership and organizational "capacity" (another word for capacity is ability). In this book and in our leadership courses it is one of the nine "Leadership Core Competencies" that all leaders should possess.

One way to strengthen that skill set over time is to follow the five "Sensemaking Implementation Practices" that Ancona outlines. You can think of these as "steps" but sense the practice of sensemaking is recursive and not strictly linear, it is helpful to think of these as "practices."

She describes them this way.

1. Explore the Wider System

It is important to listen and broadly question all internal and external stakeholders that have been identified. If the nature of the problem or change is not already explicit, then it is important to use this information to help define the issue. Formal and informal interviews, reports, social media and other online content are all valuable sources of information that can be leveraged. The data gathering process dovetails closely with relating and so provides an early opportunity to build rapport with employees.

2. Pursue opinions that differ from your own

Leaders must keep an open mind when building a sensemaking map. An important part of this is to quickly identify your own mental models and assumptions and realize how these may bias your approach to data collection. Questioning these underlying assumptions is also critical to ensuring that cognitive biases do not interfere with your sensemaking process. Leaders should delay the formation of opinions until sufficient data has been gathered, including information. from those that may disagree with his/her perspective. Never be afraid to ask, "What am I missing here?"

3. Test your assumptions

Sensemaking is an iterative process and because of this, leaders will need to evaluate their progress periodically to see if they are headed in the right direction. This is especially important when confronted with adaptive, rather than technical changes, as the nature of the solution may need to change over time as the environment changes. Once enough balanced data is gathered to form an initial hypothesis, leaders should 'learn by doing' through low-risk experiments to test their understanding and add the data gathered from these trials to their sensemaking map.

4. Adopt multiple perspectives

Try to see the issues from multiple perspectives. If a leader has reached his/her conclusions independently and the conclusions seem 'too easy' then the leader's ideas may simply be reiterating organizational stereotypes. Leaders should make use of teams and committees of key stakeholders comprising those with power, those in opposition to the change, and also those without authority (but who will be affected), to ensure their initiatives incorporate multiple perspectives. Viewing the issues from only one or two perspectives is unlikely to capture enough information for complex changes.

5. Iterate and Act

Sensemaking is an ongoing process that extends beyond just initial data gathering and implementation, but also captures feedback on the change's success after completion. As more data is obtained, a leader must update his/her map of the organization or issue and the leader's vision or invented options also refined. However, it is important for a leader not to be paralyzed by masses of data such that no action or progress is made and the initiative stalls. Therefore, once sufficient balanced information is gathered it will be me to take action and secure those early victories to help the change process gain momentum.

Drawing on Karl Weick's work around sensemaking, as well as my own experience helping C-Suite executives guide their sensemaking over the last 23 years (in my role of executive advisor, mentor and coach), I will expand on each of Ancona's five steps and elaborate further to help you identify concrete ways you can put this sensemaking skill set to work in your own department, with your current projects and with your current team.

Practice #1 - Explore the Wider System

Broadening horizons is pivotal. Leaders must continuously scan both internal and external environments to grasp the full picture. Listening, understanding, and asking questions are the primary tools at this stage.

Example:

Imagine a global tech company wanting to launch a new product. The manager doesn't just focus on his internal R&D team but also initiates dialogues with sales, customer feedback forums, competitor analysis teams, and even external technology trend analysts. By understanding varying viewpoints, from customer preferences to competitor capabilities, the manager can effectively chart the course for the product's development and positioning.

Understanding the Landscape:

At the core of any endeavor to make sense of a complex environment lies the step of exploration. Weick's concept of sensemaking emphasizes the necessity of creating a coherent, evolving map from the chaos of ambiguous events and experiences. For corporate leaders, this translates into a comprehensive understanding of both the internal and external systems.

Why Wider Exploration Matters:

Organizations do not exist in a vacuum. The intricate web of interdependencies—spanning from internal team dynamics to global economic shifts—can profoundly impact a firm's trajectory. A leader's understanding is, therefore, only as good as the breadth and depth of their exploration.

Drawing from Weick's seminal work, an organization is analogous to a brain. Just as our brain constantly updates its understanding based on sensory inputs, organizations too, via their leaders, should continually scan and interpret inputs from their environment.

Incorporating Diverse Data Points:

Formal reports, meetings, and presentations are typical avenues of information in corporate settings. However, as Weick highlights, often the most valuable insights arise from informal, unexpected, or even serendipitous interactions. Casual conversations with a junior employee might shed light on ground-level challenges, while an impromptu chat with a client might reveal market sentiments that no report captures.

Navigating Through Ambiguity:

Ambiguity is a recurring theme in Weick's work. He posits that ambiguity, rather than being an obstacle, can be a wellspring of insights if approached with curiosity. A leader's role here is not to shy away from ambiguity but to plunge into it, asking questions that help distill clarity from the unclear. For instance, suppose there's a sudden drop in a product's sales. Traditional metrics might point towards quality issues. However, by exploring the wider system, a leader might discover a range of causes: maybe there's a new competitor offering a similar product at a lower price, or perhaps there's a cultural trend moving away from the product category altogether.

Connecting with Weick's 'Grounded in Identity Construction':

Weick emphasizes that our understanding of situations is profoundly influenced by our perceived identities. In a corporate setting, this means that a leader's professional identity (e.g., a marketer, a financial expert, a technologist) can tint their interpretation of situations. Exploring the wider system challenges leaders to step out of these identity silos. A tech lead, for instance, would benefit from understanding the marketing challenges of a product, just as a CFO would gain insights from understanding on-ground operational challenges.

Synthesizing Exploration into Coherent Narratives:

Weick's work highlights the significance of constructing meaningful narratives from experiences. Exploring the wider system isn't just about gathering data—it's about weaving this data into a story that resonates, illuminates, and guides. For corporate leaders, this story becomes the bedrock of strategies and decisions. After extensive exploration, a leader might realize that their company's strength doesn't lie in competing with mainstream products but perhaps in catering to niche markets. This narrative then becomes the guiding star for future endeavors. Exploring the wider system is not a box-ticking exercise. It's an intricate dance of curiosity, resilience, and discernment. By embracing the principles highlighted by Weick—especially the value of ambiguity and the power of narrative creation—leaders can harness the vastness of their environment into actionable, insightful strategies.

Practice #2 - Pursue Opinions that Differ from Your Own

Every leader has inherent biases. The key is recognizing these biases and actively seeking out dissenting opinions. It's not about proving oneself right but about collecting diverse data points to enrich understanding.

Example:

A financial firm's CEO might favor traditional banking methods, believing they are the most reliable. However, noticing the fintech disruption, she decides to engage both with traditional bankers and new-age fintech enthusiasts in her team. By asking, "What might I be overlooking?", she learns about the emerging trends in blockchain and digital wallets, allowing her to make informed strategic decisions.

The Power of Divergent Views:

In the rapidly changing corporate environment, leaders who surround themselves with 'yes-men' or voices that only echo their own sentiments risk creating a vacuum. Divergent opinions serve as windows to new perspectives, challenges, and opportunities.

Weick's Take on Plurality:

Karl Weick's work frequently alludes to the idea that sensemaking is often a collective endeavor. He asserts that the intricacies of organizations and their ecosystems often mean that no single individual can fully grasp every nuance. Diverse voices, coming from varying backgrounds and experiences, offer a fuller, richer tapestry of the situation at hand.

Beyond the Comfort Zone:

There's a comfort in validation, in hearing what you already believe. But this comfort can be deceptive. It can stymie innovation, and at worst, lead to blind spots. Leaders should consciously engage with opinions that stretch their thinking, challenge their beliefs, and even destabilize their assumptions. For instance, in the early 2000s, the mobile phone industry leaders might have been content with the trajectory of feature phones. If they only listened to voices that affirmed the status quo, they might have missed the looming smartphone revolution. Those who engaged with the unconventional, divergent opinions were the ones who rode the wave of change.

The Pitfall of Cognitive Biases:

Our minds, in their quest for efficiency, often rely on shortcuts—cognitive biases. These biases can skew our judgment, making us favor information that aligns with our pre-existing beliefs. Actively seeking out contrasting opinions is a pragmatic approach to counteract these biases. By posing questions like, "What might I be overlooking?" or "Why do you see it differently?", leaders open doors to enlightenment.

Practical Application in Corporates:

Imagine a pharmaceutical company looking to develop a new drug. While R&D scientists might be focused on efficacy and side-effects, opinions from the sales team might highlight marketability challenges, and feedback from patient groups could reveal concerns about accessibility and affordability. The crossroads of these divergent views is where holistic solutions are birthed.

Weick's Emphasis on 'Retrospective' Sensemaking:

One of Weick's key insights is that sensemaking is often retrospective. We interpret events after they have occurred, based on the outcomes. When leaders engage with diverse opinions, they expand their retrospective horizon. They're equipped to look back not just from their viewpoint but from multiple standpoints, leading to richer, more nuanced interpretations.

Cultivate a Culture of Openness:

For this step to be genuinely effective, leaders must foster a corporate culture where divergent views are not just tolerated but celebrated. It's not enough for a leader to be open to different opinions; the entire organization should be a safe space for constructive dissent. When employees, irrespective of their hierarchy, feel empowered to voice their views, the organization transforms into a vibrant think-tank of ideas and solutions.

Challenges and the Way Forward:

Pursuing divergent opinions is not without its challenges. There's the risk of analysis paralysis, where too many opinions lead to indecision. The key is not in amassing opinions but in skillfully navigating through them, discerning the valuable insights, and integrating them into a cohesive strategy.

Pursuing opinions that differ from one's own is a journey of humility, openness, and growth. In the words of Weick, organizations are 'ongoing accomplishments that emerge from efforts to create order and make retrospective sense of what occurs'. By valuing the kaleidoscope of opinions, leaders can craft strategies that are resilient, innovative, and grounded in the collective wisdom of the organization.

Practice #3 - Test Your Assumptions

Assumptions are starting points, not conclusions. Periodically, these assumptions should undergo scrutiny. Testing them ensures that the leader's strategies stay relevant and effective.

Example:

Consider a retail company transitioning to e-commerce. Their initial assumption might be that online buyers prioritize price over brand loyalty. To test this, they launch two campaigns: one discount-driven and another focusing on brand storytelling. By analyzing the response, they discover that while discounts attract, brand narratives create returning customers. This insight would reshape their online strategy.

The Vital Role of Assumptions: Assumptions act as the invisible scaffolding upon which decisions, strategies, and actions in the corporate world are built. While they simplify complex realities, they also pose the risk of over-simplification, which can be perilous in dynamic business environments.

Enacting Environments: Karl Weick postulates that organizations don't just react to the environments but also enact or create them. In other words, by acting upon assumptions, businesses shape their reality. This feedback loop underscores the necessity to ensure assumptions are valid, relevant, and timely.

The Mechanism of Testing:

Unlike hypotheses in a scientific experiment, corporate assumptions aren't always explicitly stated. The first step is to articulate these underlying beliefs. This can be achieved through reflective practices, brainstorming sessions, or even facilitated workshops. Once laid out, each assumption needs to be scrutinized. Does market research validate the belief? Do financial trends back it up? Is there evidence within the organization – maybe in the form of past projects or initiatives – that supports or challenges the assumption? For instance, a company might assume that their customer values speed over quality. To test this, they could roll out a 'rapid delivery' version of their product, gather feedback, and assess if this aligns with their assumption.

The Value of Small-Scale Experiments:

Taking cues from agile methodologies, organizations can set up low-risk pilot projects or prototype models to test assumptions. For example, before a complete overhaul of a digital platform based on user experience assumptions, a company could make incremental changes, monitor user engagement metrics, and validate or recalibrate their beliefs.

Drawing Parallels with Weick's "Ongoing Processes":

Weick often emphasized that sensemaking is not a one-time event but an ongoing process. Similarly, testing assumptions isn't a one-off exercise. As the market, technology, and organizational dynamics evolve, so do the premises on which decisions are based. Take Nokia, for example. There was a time when their assumption – that hardware and product durability were the primary drivers of mobile phone purchases – held true. However, with the rise of smartphones and app ecosystems, this assumption quickly became outdated. Their delay in challenging and updating this belief had considerable market implications.

Challenges in the Testing Phase:

Testing can be time-consuming and resource-intensive. More subtly, it can also be threatening. Assumptions, after all, are comfort zones. Challenging them means stepping into the uncertain territory of the unknown. Corporate cultures that prioritize harmony over growth might find this process unsettling. However, as Weick's work suggests, the process of destabilizing the known is where true innovation and adaptation emerge. Leaders, therefore, need to cultivate not just the methodologies but also the mindset for rigorous assumption testing.

Feedback as a Compass:

Feedback mechanisms play a pivotal role in this process. Whether it's through analytics tools, consumer surveys, or team debriefs, feedback provides the raw data to validate or challenge assumptions.

In the world of e-commerce, A/B testing is a testament to this principle. Companies often test two versions of a webpage or advertisement, gauging consumer responses to discern which performs better. These insights then feed back into refining strategies and assumptions.

In the ever-evolving corporate landscape, standing still is tantamount to moving backward. Testing assumptions is the propeller that ensures businesses aren't just reacting to the present but shaping the future. As Weick aptly puts it, "If you can't make sense of something initially, act into it, and see if it makes sense retrospectively." This proactive, iterative approach of testing and refining is the cornerstone of adaptive, resilient businesses.

Practice #4 - Adopt Multiple Perspectives

No single viewpoint holds all answers. Leaders must approach challenges like a prism, viewing through multiple angles to discern the various patterns and solutions.

Example:

A multinational planning an expansion into Asia might view challenges from financial, cultural, and logistical angles. The finance team looks at costs, the HR team dives into cultural integration, and the operations team evaluates logistical challenges. By including representatives from each area in the decision-making committee, the CEO ensures a holistic strategy for expansion.

The Panorama of Perspectives:

In the vast tapestry of corporate life, there are a myriad of threads, each representing different stakeholder perspectives. It's not sufficient for leaders to understand just their strand. Instead, they must aim to grasp the whole picture, understanding how each thread contributes to the larger design.

Weick's Assertion on the Social Context:

Sensemaking, as conceived by Karl Weick, is not a solitary endeavor. He often stressed the importance of the social context in shaping our understanding. The idea isn't just to gather varied perspectives but to understand the conditions and contexts from which these viewpoints emerge. Doing so offers a depth of insight unparalleled by solitary analysis.

Why Multiple Perspectives Matter:

Simply put, no one has a monopoly on knowledge or insight. In the corporate realm, a marketing team might understand consumer behavior, but they might lack insights into operational logistics that the supply chain team possesses. Conversely, the tech team might be proficient in software nuances but might not have a grasp of on-ground sales challenges. Take the example of the launch of a new digital product. While the tech team ensures smooth functioning, the design team ensures user-friendliness, marketing ensures it reaches the target audience, and customer support anticipates potential issues users might face. The product's success lies at the intersection of all these perspectives.

Benefits of a Multi-faceted Approach:

a) Risk Mitigation: By viewing issues from various angles, potential pitfalls can be identified and addressed before they escalate.

b) Innovation Stimulation: Different viewpoints can lead to the cross-pollination of ideas, birthing innovative solutions.

c) Stakeholder Engagement: When everyone feels heard and their perspectives valued, it fosters a culture of engagement and ownership.

Practical Ways to Engage Multiple Perspectives:

a) Cross-functional Teams: Creating teams with members from different departments can ensure varied viewpoints are considered. For instance, when a retail brand is launching a new outlet, representatives from real estate, operations, marketing, and sales can come together to offer a holistic view.

b) Stakeholder Interviews: Regular interactions with external stakeholders, like suppliers, customers, or industry experts, can provide invaluable external perspectives.

c) Feedback Platforms: Tools like suggestion boxes, feedback forums, or town hall meetings can serve as platforms where employees at all levels can voice their insights.

The Value of Redundancy:

While some might argue that having multiple perspectives can lead to redundant information, Weick saw redundancy as valuable. It acts as a form of validation. If different departments or stakeholders voice similar concerns or highlight similar trends, it underlines the importance of that particular piece of information.

Challenges and Navigating Them:

Adopting multiple perspectives doesn't come without challenges. It can lead to information overload, and conflicting viewpoints might cause paralysis by analysis. However, the goal isn't to act on every perspective but to use them as a lens, refining and adjusting one's understanding. Leaders need to master the art of synthesis, distilling vast amounts of information into actionable insights. They need to strike a balance between being inclusive of different perspectives and being decisive in action.

In the intricate dance of corporate decision-making, multiple perspectives serve as the different dance steps. Each step, while distinct, contributes to the elegance and effectiveness of the dance. Weick's emphasis on the social nature of sensemaking serves as a timely reminder for leaders. By consciously weaving in diverse perspectives, they not only enhance the robustness of their decisions but also foster a culture of inclusivity, collaboration, and mutual respect.

Practice #5 - Iterate and Act

Sensemaking is dynamic. As new data surfaces, leaders should be ready to adjust their maps and strategies. But equally crucial is the courage to act on acquired knowledge without getting bogged down by the quest for perfection.

Example:

A software development company after initial testing releases a beta version of their app to a select group. They gather feedback, refine, and relaunch iteratively. While the quest for the perfect app continues, they understand the importance of market presence and user feedback, ensuring they aren't paralyzed by the weight of information.

The Iterative Dance of Progress:

While the first four steps of the sensemaking process lay a solid foundation for understanding the environment, the final step— Iterate and Act— translates this understanding into concrete, impactful actions. It embodies the essence of Weick's view on sensemaking: understanding is not just a precursor to action; it is intertwined with it. By acting, organizations not only impact their environment but also refine their understanding of it, therefore it should be seen as recursive and iterative.

Sensemaking in Motion:

Sensemaking, especially as depicted by Karl Weick, isn't a linear process where one moves from ignorance to understanding in a singular, straightforward progression. Instead, it's cyclical— organizations act based on their current understanding, gather feedback, and then refine their actions and understanding in tandem.

Feedback Loops as Navigational Aids:

In a corporate environment, feedback loops act as the GPS, helping organizations navigate the tumultuous terrains of the market. For instance, a software company might release a new application feature based on initial sensemaking. User feedback on this feature, both positive and critical, becomes crucial data for further sensemaking, determining future refinements or even entirely new directions.

Small Steps, Big Gains:

The notion of "acting" doesn't always imply sweeping changes or grand gestures. Often, it's about small, calculated steps—pilot projects, prototype launches, or targeted campaigns. These modest initiatives allow companies to gauge market reactions without committing extensive resources. They exemplify the agile principle of "failing fast" and "learning faster." Consider a company like Amazon. Their approach to launching new services or features often involves testing them in select markets or with specific user groups. Feedback from these smaller segments informs larger, more widespread rollouts.

The Danger of Paralysis:

While the iterative approach emphasizes reflection and refinement, it's essential to strike a balance. There's a potential pitfall—paralysis by analysis. Continual reflection shouldn't become an excuse for inaction. Leaders need to discern when they have "enough" information to act, even if it's not "complete" information. This is particularly pertinent in fast-evolving industries where waiting for complete clarity might mean missing out on crucial opportunities.

Learning from Missteps:

Iterative action also means that not every action will hit the mark. Some initiatives will falter. However, in the spirit of sensemaking, even these missteps offer value—they're rich sources of data, teaching organizations about market dynamics, internal capabilities, or unforeseen challenges. A classic example is the story of New Coke. In the mid-1980s, Coca-Cola, based on various data points, decided to reformulate its iconic beverage. The backlash was swift and severe. However, the company's quick response to revert to the original formula and the lessons they learned about brand loyalty and consumer sentiment turned a potential disaster into a testament to adaptive, responsive leadership.

Retrospective Sensemaking:

One of Karl Weick's seminal contributions to the sensemaking discourse is the idea that sensemaking is often retrospective. Organizations act, see the outcomes, and then make sense of these actions in hindsight. This retrospective lens is vital because it emphasizes that sensemaking doesn't end once action is initiated. The outcomes of actions, in turn, become inputs for further sensemaking.

Institutionalizing Iterative Sensemaking:

For organizations to truly harness the power of iterative sensemaking, it can't be an ad-hoc effort. Systems and processes need to be in place to gather feedback, assess outcomes, and channel these insights back into the decision-making pipeline. Regular review meetings, feedback collection mechanisms, and a culture that values both successes and constructive failures are essential.

"Acting" in the sensemaking process is not just the culmination—it's an integral part of the journey. It's through actions and their outcomes that organizations fine-tune their understanding, adapt to shifting circumstances, and carve their path forward. Weick's insights serve as a beacon, reminding leaders that in the complex dance of understanding and action, every step, every move, every leap, and every fall is an opportunity to learn, grow, and make better sense of the world around them.

Conclusion

In corporate ecosystems, sensemaking is not a luxury—it's a necessity. Ancona's steps, when practiced with dedication, equip leaders to decipher the enigmatic, act with conviction, and steer their teams through the uncertain terrains of the corporate world.

From understanding diverse perspectives to constantly re-evaluating their stance, leaders who embrace sensemaking are not just reactors to change but architects of the future. In the words of Ancona, it's about understanding the "as is" to navigate towards the "to be". Whether you're launching a new product, restructuring your organization, or entering new markets, the compass of sensemaking will guide you to success.

As a leader, the better you get at this skill of sensemaking, the better you will be able to serve, influence, and help "steer your organization across a continuously changing landscape toward the shared vision, shared goals and ultimately, the desired destination.

The next skill set that all effective leaders demonstrate competency in is "Stakeholder Alignment." This is the domain of vision, purpose, values and directional statements, and is the focus of the next chapter.

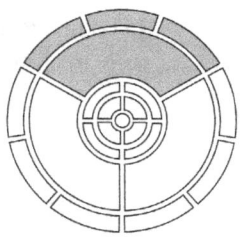

CHAPTER 7: STAKEHOLDER ALIGNMENT

First, we begin with a clear definition and the benchmarks for levels of proficiency in this skill set. I define Stakeholder Alignment skill set as establishing vision, values and purpose, and aligning interests of stakeholders for mutual commitment. This skill set is concerned with your ability to establish and articulate your organization's direction in the form of vision, values and purpose, then to align all key stakeholders so that they will feel a shared commitment and be able to demonstrate it.

Team Discussion

When you initiate a conversation with your employees and team(s), you could use some version of the following questions.

- How do we establish and articulate our organization's direction in the form of vision statements?

- How do we clarify and reinforce organizational values and purpose?

- How do we align our key stakeholders to the organization's direction and cultivate shared commitment?

Benchmarks

Next we move into the benchmarks for this skill set.

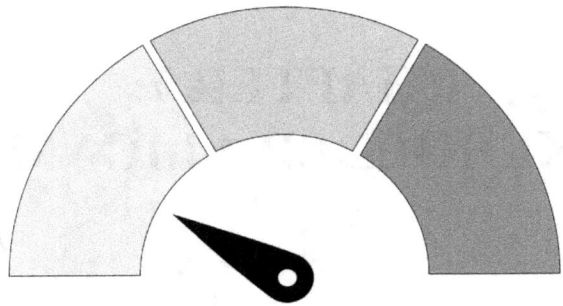

STAKEHOLDER ALIGNMENT LOWER RANGE

A leader and a team functioning in the lower range of proficiency in this skill set might describe it this way.

Leadership has shared the vision with the employees, however, we haven't invested a lot into things like core values or articulating the purpose of the organization. We talk to the key stakeholders but haven't implemented any kind of formal process to "align their interests" or achieve shared commitment. Overall stakeholder commitment to the organization's direction ranges from medium to low.

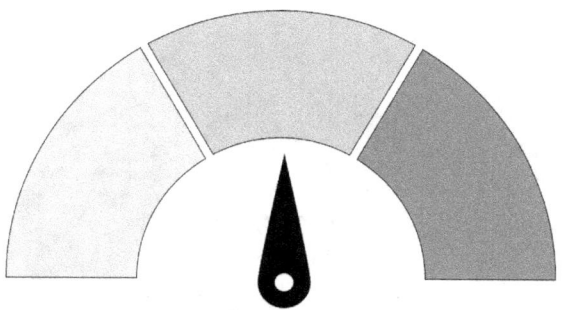

STAKEHOLDER ALIGNMENT INTERMEDIATE RANGE

A leader and a team functioning in the intermediate range of proficiency in this skill set might describe it this way.

Leadership has invested time clarifying the organizational vision, our core values and our purpose. We do talk to the key stakeholders to try to understand their needs. However, the level of buy-in and commitment to our vision, values and purpose is inconsistent. We need to do a better job of enrolling everyone for a shared commitment (and we may consider taking a fresh look at our vision, values and purpose).

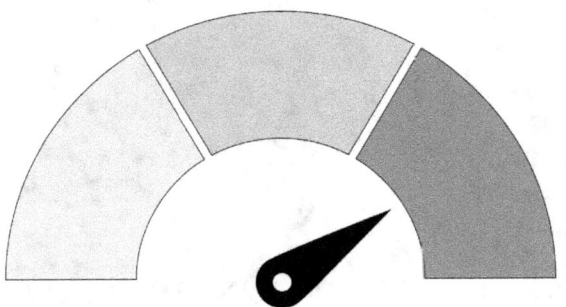

STAKEHOLDER ALIGNMENT I HIGHER RANGE

A leader and a team functioning in the higher range of proficiency in this skill set might describe it this way.

We have well-articulated vision, core values and purpose statements and our culture (including mindsets and behaviors) are aligned with them. We are strong believers in understanding our stakeholders' needs and weave their perspectives and interests into our plans. We enjoy high levels of commitment across most of our stakeholders which is reflected in high levels of support, cooperation, and consistently impressive results.

Putting Stakeholder Alignment into Perspective

Stakeholder Alignment is also called "Organizational alignment." It is fundamentally about ensuring that all parts of an organization are working cohesively towards common goals and that the strategy, people, processes, and culture are in sync. It's about optimizing the organization to effectively achieve its mission and vision. Directional statements, such as vision, values, and purpose statements, are pivotal tools for leaders to shape culture, set direction, and guide decision-making.

Directional Statements

Directional statements serve as organizational compasses, guiding a company's strategic decisions and cultural behaviors. The *vision* statement paints an aspirational picture of the organization's desired future; the *values* statement outlines core beliefs and principles dictating its actions and behaviors; and the *purpose* statement defines the fundamental reason for the organization's existence beyond mere profit generation. Collectively, these statements anchor an organization's identity, clarifying its direction and shaping its ethos for stakeholders.

Benefits of Stakeholder Alignment:

Shaping Culture: These statements provide a shared understanding of what the organization stands for, thereby influencing behavior and decision-making.

Setting Direction: They offer a clear direction to ensure that efforts are coordinated and not wasted.

Stakeholder Commitment: They help build trust, loyalty, and commitment among stakeholders, including employees, customers, and investors.

Strategic Decision-Making: With alignment, decisions can be made more quickly, with less ambiguity, because there's a shared understanding of the goals and values.

Key Principles & Practices:

Engagement: Involve employees and stakeholders in the process of developing vision, values, and purpose statements. This fosters ownership and buy-in.

Communication: Regularly communicate the vision, values, and purpose to ensure they remain top of mind and are fully integrated into the organization's DNA.

Modeling: Leaders should exemplify the values and vision in their behavior. It's not just about stating them; it's about living them.

Reinforcement: Use performance management, rewards, and recognition systems to reinforce desired behaviors aligned with the vision and values. Review & Refresh: Regularly review and, if necessary, refresh these statements to ensure they remain relevant as the organization evolves.

Vision

Vision plays a central role in leadership. When you think of vision, you probably think about a "vision for the future". The element of time is important as we consider vision. We are envisioning a better future than we have today. We envision a future that reflects growth, improvement, and/or change.

The very concept and practice of leadership presupposes movement from one place (actual or metaphorical) to another. When we add movement to the element of time, we can imagine that over time, we journey to and arrive at a new destination of some kind. That new destination is the vision.

It answers the question that the followers ask the leader implicitly or explicitly, "Where are we going?" This "movement" could include growing from a new department, team or business unit to being a success group or division of the institution.

The movement could be shifting from a team or work unit being ineffective or troubled in some way to working very well together, and being viewed as highly successful. Or movement could be some kind of large-scale organizational transformation, where the institution changes how it operates in some fundamental way, or transforms its culture over time.

In every case, movement implies a destination of sorts. People can be ordered to move in a certain direction, but taking an external top-down approach to directing movement has significant limitations.

Among them includes the fact that when you order change, you often get compliance but not commitment. While compliance is useful and necessary, it is usually not sufficient for team and organizational success. This is particularly true of younger workers, who are less responsive to purely command-and-control management styles.

Vision vs. Strategy

Strategy is crucial, but it is not very inspirational. Strategies inform managers of what to do and, in some cases, how to do it. But they do not address why they should do it.

Leaders must go beyond the what and how and create an organization that members can identify with, take pride in and commit to. Doing so requires vision rather than strategy.

Vision vs. Goals

Goals are analytical and appeal to the logical, linear left brain. Vision is an imagined destination, it is less tangible than goals.

Vision contains goals, but is larger than goals. You could say that vision "paints a picture". Leaders express their vision for the future through a narrative, such as a story about what the future will be like, or by painting a picture with words and compelling descriptions. Vision touches the heart, not just the mind.

Defining Vision

We define vision as "a compelling description of a desired future state". At its essence, vision is imagination plus courage.

Karl Albrecht calls it "A shared image of what we want the enterprise to be or become. It provides an aiming point for a future orientation. It answers the question, 'How do we want those we care about to perceive us?'"

Burt Nanus describes a vision as "A realistic, credible, attractive future for your organization … an idea so energizing that it, in effect, jump-starts the future by calling forth the skills, talents, and resources to make it happen … and a signpost pointing the way for all who need to understand what the organization is and where it intends to go.

Warren Blank likens a vision to "A unique wide-angle and long-range lens of awareness [that enables people] to see into the future and to comprehend big-picture possibilities."

Vision Transcends and Includes

Management literature often discusses vision as an enterprise-level exercise. However, it would be a mistake to think of vision as something that belongs only in the boardroom. It is not enough for vision to only be occurring at the most senior levels of leadership. It is necessary that the most senior levels of leadership offer some kind of destination, some kind of vision for the future. It is also important to socialize the vision in the organization so that it becomes a shared vision.

The best way for people to share a vision is to give them an opportunity to contribute, in meaningful ways, to bringing that future vision into reality. This means that they need to be able to see clearly, and to understand, how their work and effort contributes to not only the present success of the organization, but also helps move it closer to its vision. Better yet, each division leader, department leader and team leader should be encouraged to create a vision for their unit, and how they can improve their area of operation, in ways that support the larger vision.

In this way, vision is happening at every level of the organization. You can think of these visions as nested circles. The departmental vision fits into the functional area vision, and the functional area's vision, in turn, fits into the overall vision of the company.

Qualities of a Good Vision

1. A good vision offers team members a view of the future that is clearly and demonstrably better than the present.

2. A good vision evokes a clear and positive mental image of the desired future state. Put another way, it paints a clear picture.

3. A good vision creates an emotional response by appealing to the right side of the brain (the domain of images and feelings).

4. A good vision clarifies direction and focuses attention.

5. A good vision is meaningful in the context of the institution's purpose, values, capabilities, and circumstances.

6. A good vision is motivating and memorable.

7. A good vision inspires commitment and encourages enthusiasm.

8. A good vision emphasizes the most important factors (for the future) and screens out the nonessential ones.

9. A good vision bridges the present and future while moving people to action (pushing beyond comfort zones).

10. A good vision respects the past and is rooted in the realities of employees, stakeholders (customers or community members), and the broader industry, supply chain, or society.

11. A good vision reflects those things that the institution and its leaders deem most important and about which they are most passionate about.

12. A good vision is related to the organization's genuine competencies— those things at which it can be the best. (Here organization could be division, department, work unit or team.)

Leaders can use vision statements—in various formats—to communicate, to evangelize, to get buy-in from key stakeholders, to establish a shared vision, and to reinforce vision over time. Traditionally, vision statements have taken the form of a sentence, a short paragraph, or even a manifesto. Today, some leaders use agency-produced "commercials" or documentary-style videos to convey their vision.

Whatever form they take, vision statements are only pointers to the vision. They serve as a proxy, a touchstone to connect people with the imagined future. The important thing is the impact the vision has on the listener (or viewer or reader).

To efficiently evangelize their vision, leaders should have enough clarity to convey the vision in a concise, compelling "elevator pitch."

Developing Vision Descriptions and Vision Statements

Your vision for the future of your division, department or unit can be conveyed in a myriad of ways. Many leaders write multi-page descriptions of how they imagine and envision the future of their enterprise. Known as "vision descriptions," these long documents can be extremely helpful as the leader clarifies thoughts and ideas and experiments with various ways of conveying the vision to different audiences.

It is impractical, however, for every stakeholder to read and internalize all the nuances of these long documents. A single sentence or short paragraph description of a vision is known as a "vision statement."

Management experts offer various formulas and templates for constructing vision statements. These guidelines can provide a conceptual framework for an ambiguous task akin to creating art. But in trying to use a step-by-step process to create a vision statement, many leaders fall into the "vision versus vision statement" trap.

Do not confuse "vision" with "vision statements." These are two very different things. Having a vision statement does not mean that you have vision.

The vision statement is useful only as a pointer—a mnemonic device—to help people remember, reconnect with, and reinforce the vision. The vision statement is a verbal representation of your vision for the future.

No formula or template can generate your vision for the future. No amount of wordsmithing or fancy editing can substitute for a leader's genuine vision.

Putting forth an unimaginative vision statement may diminish a leader's credibility.

If you have not found your vision, then refrain from offering a vision statement that will only underscore this fact. Visioning itself can be painstaking and time-consuming. Or the inspiration of vision may arise with complete spontaneity, without conscious effort and just come to you in a moment of clarity.

No step-by-step process can explain how Churchill conceived his "Britain's finest hour" vision. No template can reverse-engineer Disney's process for inventing his Disneyland vision or Martin Luther King's inspiration for his "I Have a Dream" speech.

Leadership author Jay Conger describes the vision creation process as "a fragmented, evolutionary… largely intuitive [and] incremental ... creative process." He calls the process "murky and uncertain."

Burt Nanus, author of the book, Visionary Leadership, describes the process as "messy, introspective, and difficult to explain, even for the person who conceives the vision."

A leader's vision is as unique as that leader's beliefs, passions, and ambitions. The way each person becomes inspired is also unique, and the same applies to a group, department, or organization.

Organizational Vision vs. Personal Vision

An inspired view of the future, of what can be, of what we can be, comes from deep within. People with little passion have little vision.

Vision comes from inspiration. How deep is the well you draw your inspiration from?

As a leader, you are encouraged to cultivate greater clarity about your own personal values, your own sense of purpose in your life, and a personal vision for yourself before you try to craft an inspired vision for your organization (your division, department, or team). The better you know yourself, what is most important to you, and what you are most passionate about, the deeper the well from which you can draw inspiration from.

As a leader, you are strongly encouraged to invest the necessary time and introspection to identify your own personal vision for your life and career.

Where do you see yourself, ideally, in 10 years? Five years? Three years?

As a leader of your unit, department or division, you are also encouraged to draw on the guidelines offered in this lesson and begin to explore how your longer-term goals can be subsumed into a broader, more compelling vision of the future.

The shared vision you and your fellow leaders create for your group will not only provide direction (answering the question, "Where are we going?") but also provide inspiration for the people who in your organization.

Values

Values are a primary way that managers and leaders can create meaning, motivate employees, and influence culture. In this part of the book, we will explore the values of the leader and also the values of the organization. Later in this book, in the chapter on Meaningful Motivation, we will look at other people's values (especially the values of your employees and team members whom you want to influence and motivate).

Let's start with the basics. So, what exactly are values?

Every human being naturally seeks the desirable and avoids the unpleasant. But one individual may experience a given set of circumstances as exhilarating, while another – in exactly the same situation — may experience it as terrifying.

One person may perceive an object as inspiring, while another may find the same object offensive. Why do different people assign such wildly different meanings to the same facts, circumstances, and experiences? The answer, of course, is values.

The word value comes from the word evaluation. Human values are subconscious, conditioned "evaluations" of subjective experience.

Values are a primary way that humans, including all of the people who report to you, make meaning.

And, as we will see, values are also a primary tool of highly skilled managers and leaders who know how to motivate and influence people.

Perceptual Filters

Values are perceptual filters people use to determine (to evaluate) what is important in any given situation or circumstance.

In terms of understanding what people care about, in terms of knowing what motivates people, in terms of understanding people in the most fundamental sense, few things are more significant than values.

Oddly enough, for most people, including most managers and leaders, values are invisible. Many people assume that others think and "evaluate" the same way they do.

This explains why most leaders find it easy to understand and motivate some people—the people who have the same values as they do—yet are completely perplexed by other people (who they will describe as unmotivated or "those who don't get it").

Each person has a different life experience, in different life circumstances, and often in different environments. Over a lifetime, a person has millions of experiences.

The mind catalogs each experience as pleasant or unpleasant, desirable or undesirable, safe or unsafe, and attractive or unattractive. In other words, a person's "value system" is the mechanism their mind uses to evaluate subjective experience and arrive at actionable conclusions (that can inform choices and behavior).

Our values act as "perceptual filters" that help us distinguish the various shades of meaning related to what we like and do not like.

Values are generalizations about subjective experience. Without these generalizations, we would have to evaluate every single experience in painstaking detail to determine whether it was good, wholesome, and desirable or tenuous, suspicious, and dangerous—which would, of course, be paralyzing.

Our value system comprises thousands of generalizations and assumptions that our minds have accumulated and synthesized over decades, equipping us to quickly size up a situation or experience and recognize that as something that either resonates with or violates one or more of our values.

This gives us a nearly instant read on objects, people, behavior, circumstances, experiences, and choices.

We instantly feel attracted to, resonant with, motivated by, or even inspired by certain people, cultures, management, and leadership styles without having to stop and evaluate each detail.

Similarly, we may feel put off by certain people, cultures, management or leadership styles just as quickly, and always without having to consciously think about it or evaluate the details.

These feelings of resonance and attraction, or a feeling of aversion or distaste is largely a function of our values.

Interestingly, some people haven't spent a lot of time reflecting on their values. In other words, for many people, their values are largely subconscious.

As we will see, values play a central role in motivation, decision-making, perceived trust and credibility, team and organizational culture, and especially influence.

Values Research

Values influence almost every aspect of our lives: our choices, our responses to others, our aesthetic preferences, our objectives, and our sense of ethics and morality. Our values (and values systems) motivate us before we achieve a goal. Values also determine how satisfied we will feel once we attain a given goal. Our value system determines which people and cultures we are resonant with (and which we find off-putting).

Our values also determine which managers and leaders (and styles) employees are naturally resonant with (or instantly dislike).

The use of "values models" is widespread in business and academia and has informed dozens of distinct models that differ in details but are quite similar in principle and overarching conclusions. Values research has been widely used by psychologists, political scientists, and marketers for decades.

The pervasive role of values in all aspects of human life has motivated hundreds of studies in the disciplines of consumer behavior, psychology, sociology, and cultural-anthropology.

A large body of research has shown conclusively that values represent both a powerful explanation of and influence on a variety of individual and collective behaviors. In fact, in recent years, the study of values has become one of the most dynamic research areas in the social science disciplines.

Several values analysis methodologies are currently available, and more are surfacing.

For purposes of this values primer, we will stay focused on some of the most fundamental aspects of values and value systems, and how we can use this understanding to be better leaders.

Never Confuse Goals with Values

Many well-intentioned leaders and managers focus on goal setting.

Goal setting has its place in organizational life. In other sections we explore the importance of setting targets.

However, as important as goals are, it is also important to realize that goal setting has only a limited impact on people's motivation (and even less impact on emotional satisfaction or fulfillment).

Goals are certainly useful for establishing targets and milestones and guiding actions toward hitting those targets. However, for most employees, the sense of meaning, satisfaction and motivation does not come from the goals themselves, but rather, the values that the goals either represent or promise to satisfy.

Simply put, goals are what we want and values are what we think and feel is important.

We associate goals with targets or desired outcomes. We associate values with what is important to us. What we value. What we care about. What we see as high priority.

Think of it this way. Achieving a goal is essentially hitting a target. But what is important and significant about hitting that target? Perhaps hitting that target makes our company better positioned to fend off aggressive competitor actions? Perhaps achieving that goal means that we can purchase better protective gear for our security officers? Then safety is the value underlying these very different goals. People are far more motivated by the value of safety than the idea of achieving a goal.

Goals are useful as targets to aim toward as we work to bring our external reality into alignment with our internal values.

Put another way, we can use goals to affect our external world to better satisfy our values. But it would be a mistake to think that the goals offer any satisfaction. The emotional satisfaction, the sense of meaning, the sense of fulfillment comes from the values that underlie or are represented by the goal.

When we adopt other people's goals, we sometimes experience disappointment when we achieve the goal but it does not satisfy any of our own intrinsic values.

This is why some people work very hard over many months or years to accomplish a goal but feel disappointed or even empty when that achievement doesn't feel very satisfying.

The implication here for us managers and leaders, is that if we want our goals to mean anything to the people who report to us, we need to frame the goals in terms of the values that the goals represent.

Also, each person is primarily motivated by their own values, not someone else's. So, it is important that you get to know the people who report to you and learn what they value.

Values are the primary form of motivation for people. Once you learn what they value, you will then know what motivates them. You have undoubtedly noticed this in your own life over many years of setting and accomplishing goals. If you reflect back, you will see that the goals that were unsatisfying to you were those not based on your values.

Truly satisfying goals are those that reflect and express your core values. This is also true for people in your organization.

Perhaps you have noticed that some employees did not seem motivated by some departmental goals, and even once they accomplish those goals, they seem to derive little to no satisfaction from the achievement.

That is because goals do little to motivate (most people) and offer even less in terms of fulfillment after they are accomplished.

Most of the motivation of completing the goal and all of the fulfillment that comes after the goal is accomplished, are derived from the underlying values, not the goal itself. This has numerous implications for you as a manager and leader. The first is that you must understand what people care about.

If you want to know how to motivate an employee, you need to know what is important to them (their values).

Clarifying Your Own Values as a Leader

To feel truly successful and fulfilled in life, a person needs to be living their values. This is especially true for leaders.

This can be difficult for many since they don't know what their values are, or may have adopted the values of their parents or traditions without spending a lot of time thinking about those values and reflecting for themselves if those values are a good fit to their own life's vision.

What matters most to you?

Core values are the answer to the question, "What is most enduringly important to me?"

They are the deep values that influence what we see, whom we choose to interact with, and how we behave.

When we violate our core values, we feel guilty or disappointed or feel we have let ourselves down in some way. But when our actions align with our core values, we are proud and work with a clear conscience.

The values that underlie individual and team goals provide you a crucial key to motivating your team and creating a motivating culture.

As a leader, it is an excellent idea to write down your top 10-15 "core values" and spend some time editing your descriptions and maybe prioritizing the values for your own vision of your life.

What is most important to you?

What are your highest priorities? What values bring you the most satisfaction in life?

Values clarification is a way to consciously define success and meaning in your own terms. If you spend some time writing down your core values, you may notice that different dimensions of life each have a set of values that motivate you. For example, you could ask, "What is most important to me in my career?" That would help you uncover some of your career values.

Similarly, you might ask, "What is most important to me about my family and relationships?" That question would elicit a list of family and relationship values.

Many leaders spend time crafting a "Core Values Statement" for themselves. Core values are living behavioral guidelines that act as sentries, subconsciously scanning the horizon for information relevant to our core concerns and priorities.

Different values influence different parts of our actions depending on what we are doing, where we are, and whom we are with.

Through these filters, our minds create information from raw sensory data and send that information up the chain of conscious decision-making. Data with no relevance to our core values is much less likely to be considered for action. Because our core values determine what we pay attention to attention to and act on, it is essential that they be both coherent and comprehensive.

If our core values ignore an essential dimension of life (e.g., relationships, ethics, or personal growth), then we will have a blind spot adversely affecting how we live and work.

This underscores the importance of being clear, and also being explicit about what we value the most.

In this next section we will shift from a focus on our own values, the values of the people who report to us, and also the values of the people we interact with in the communities we serve.

The previous distinction between goals and values has a significant implication for your own career and life satisfaction. Your values determine your fulfillment. Until you have clearly defined your core values, it is highly unlikely you will achieve deep and lasting fulfillment from either your professional or personal life.

In fact, many people discover that they've spent a decade or more pursuing goals they adopted from a parent, society, or some tradition that was not resonant with any of their own real values. This is a very unpleasant experience that is sometimes called "disillusionment".

This underscores the importance of clarifying values before setting goals. Success without fulfillment is fool's gold. Success that is unfulfilling cannot be considered by a reasonable person to be true success.

We all know people who have the trappings of success (title, income, home, car) but are deeply unsatisfied, deeply unhappy. Only people with a rudimentary understanding of values consider those material achievements as true success.

To feel truly successful, a person needs to be living their values.

This is difficult for many since they don't know what their values are, or merely adopted the values of their parents or traditions without ever deciding for themselves if those values were right for them. Values clarification is a way to consciously define success in your own terms. And not only success, you can also define career, family, relationships, parenting, and what spirituality means to you, in your own terms. Core values are living behavioral guidelines that act as sentries, subconsciously scanning the horizon for information relevant to our core concerns and priorities.

Different values influence different parts of our actions depending on what we are doing, where we are, and whom we are with. Through these filters, our minds create information from raw sensory data and send that information up the chain of conscious decision-making. Data with no relevance to our core values is much less likely to be considered for action. Because our core values determine what we pay attention to and act on, it is essential that they be both coherent and comprehensive.

If our core values ignore an essential dimension of life (e.g., relationships, ethics, or personal growth), then we will have a blind spot adversely affecting how we live and work.

What matters most?

Core values are the answer to the question, "What is most enduringly important to me?"

They are the deep values that influence what we see, whom we choose to interact with, and how we behave. When we violate our core values, we feel guilty or disappointed or feel we have let ourselves down in some way. But when our actions align with our core values, we feel pride and work with a clear conscience. The values that underlie individual and team goals provide you a crucial key to motivating your team and creating a motivating culture.

Walking the Talk

Credibility is the "currency" of leadership. Followers naturally gravitate toward leaders who are credible, who have integrity, and who behave in a way that seems consistent with their values and beliefs—in other words, when there is little gap between their walk (actions) and their talk (their espoused values).

Leaders who "walk their talk" are viewed as trustworthy. Leaders who do not are viewed as untrustworthy. When there is a significant gap between a leader's walk (actions) and talk (values), they are perceived by others to be less trustworthy. As we navigate the intricacies of life and work, we often encounter troublesome complexities, moral dilemmas, and competing priorities. Priorities and values often run counter to and sometimes directly conflict with one another. It's not easy to always walk our talk.

Organizational Values

Many of the insights about individual values (and guiding principles) apply equally at the group or organizational level. Organizational values (whether for a project team, department, management team, or entire company) determine priorities, motivation, goals, and ultimately, satisfaction level.

A leader who has not learned to unearth and influence group values is a long way from being able to engage organizational meaning with skill or precision. Cultures are made up of a combination of values and practices. When you list the values of a group, you are essentially describing that group's culture.

In the same way that individuals benefit from a clear sense of core values, organizations benefit from clearly defined core values and guiding principles. Values are an essential part of the underlying dynamics that shape how people think, feel, and behave in organizations.

The Disney company's values of imagination and wholesomeness did not stem from market requirements; rather, they were derived from the founder's inner belief that imagination and wholesomeness should be nurtured for their own sake. William Procter and James Gamble instilled in the culture of Procter & Gamble a focus on product excellence as not merely a strategy for success, but as an almost religiously held tenet. Service to the customer, even to the point of subservience, is a way of life at Nordstrom, tracing back to its roots in 1901.

For Herb Kelleher, founder of Southwest Airlines, positively-outrageous customer service and fun were deep personal values; he did not get them from a book or hear them from a management guru. Ralph S. Larsen, former CEO of Johnson & Johnson, put it this way: "The core values embodied in our credo might be a competitive advantage, but that is not why we have them. We have them because they define for us what we stand for, and we would hold them even if they became a competitive disadvantage in certain situations.

In her book, "Meaning Is the New Money," author Tammy Ericson points out, "My research has clearly shown that high levels of engagement, and the associated discretionary effort, occur when our work experiences reflect a clear set of values that we share … It's what people are looking for at work. Clear company values, translated into the day-to- day work experience, are one of the strongest drivers of an engaged workforce, one primed for successful collaboration."

Previously, we explored the challenge of leaders having to consistently walk the talk. The same difficulties arise within organizations.

For example, healthcare delivery organizations must constantly juggle the competing values of "providing easy access to care," "keeping care affordable," and "providing the highest quality of care possible."

All these values are essential to customer safety and satisfaction, but concrete decisions (such as a satellite clinic's hours and staffing) cannot possibly maximize each value as though in a vacuum.

In the real world, what we consider optimal is more often a matter of maintaining a dynamic balance between several essential considerations rather than seeking to emphasize a single priority.

The capacity to consciously and gracefully handle competing commitments —a hallmark of psychological maturity—separates leaders from managers and companies that scale and stay true to their values from companies that do not.

Having a clear sense of organizational core values (especially when articulated as "guiding principles") can be extremely helpful as leaders nurture the culture they want and guide employee attitudes and behaviors.

Organizational guiding principles can be a touchstone that helps managers and employees navigate hiring, onboarding, training, feedback, performance reviews, and making difficult strategy decisions. They also provide a way for employees who are a "good cultural fit" to plug in and feel at home, and help team members who don't share the company's values (and stand out "like a sore thumb") to recognize the lack of fit and move on to find a more suitable culture.

Guidelines, Attitudes, and Behavior

To grow, a company must develop ways to engage complex types of work efficiently and effectively. It must distribute throughout the organization the experience and expertise of its founders, leaders, and specialists. Today's knowledge workers thrive in an environment of information and autonomy where general guidelines are offered along with the freedom to find and implement the best approach or solution and to adapt as circumstances change.

Policies and procedures are often used as the primary mechanism to influence behavior. Policy can influence behavior in the sense that it addresses "micro behaviors."

In certain areas where every aspect of employee behavior and decisions can be anticipated, programmed for, regimented, and enforced (such as on assembly lines or in entry-level manual labor functions), using policy (and punishment or reward to ensure compliance) may suffice. But most workers in today's organizations use their minds, not just their hands, to do their jobs, and for these knowledge workers, policy is insufficient to adequately inform them on how to do their jobs.

This is because policy tells workers only what to do in the most tangible sense. Policy does not tell workers how to do it (the intangible).

Is it enough that employees of Four Seasons Resorts answer guests' questions politely? That is a tangible policy. Successful guest service representatives at Four Seasons bend over backward, not because a policy dictates the details of every interaction, but because they understand how Four Seasons treats their guests. They understand the intangible attitudes that constitute the "Four Seasons Way." Developing a coherent set of core values or guiding principles enables an organization's employees to adopt guidelines for making decisions that are aligned with the knowledge and experience of the organization's leadership.

This alleviates the need to create detailed policies and procedures to address every possible contingency. Shared core values enable even a very large group of people to function in a coordinated manner, even though each person and business unit is free to act autonomously to accomplish their objectives.

Don't all companies basically value the same things? Then why bother?

People who don't understand values might criticize the process of clarifying and conveying core values by saying, "Everyone has the same core values: excellence, customer service, success, growth, caring about people, and so on. So why waste our time making a list of words that are the same as every other values statement?"

All organizations absolutely do not value the same things. Some leaders have thrown together a "values statement" with little thought, but a values statement that genuinely reflects the priorities of a group will be as unique as the individuals who make up that group.

It is reasonable to say that most business people value customer service, product excellence, and success. But how and why they prioritize those and other aspects of their business will differ greatly from group to group. It is irrelevant if an organization's values statement seems similar to others, because values statements are not advertisements and are not in competition with one another. Values serve the people to whom they belong. For the record, not all companies list customer service as a core value. Sony, for example, does not. Not all companies list quality as a core value; Walmart does not. Not all companies list teamwork as a core value; Nordstrom does not. And not all values have to be nice-sounding, politically correct phrases reminiscent of cookie-cutter values statements created by unimaginative, unengaged leadership teams.

To keep this book in the series a reasonable length, I will reserve in-depth discussion of the additional topics of "purpose" as well as the detailed descriptions of practices that effective leaders use to clarify, articulate and align these components (vision, values, purpose).

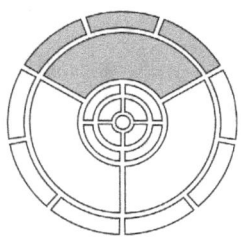

CHAPTER 8: ORGANIZATIONAL STEERING

First, we begin with a clear definition and the benchmarks for levels of proficiency in this skill set. This skill set is all about strategic thinking and planning and prioritizing according to leverage. It is concerned with your ability to develop and evolve organizational strategies, establish and revise goals, objectives, and plans, and prioritize the highest-leverage projects that will lead to the desired outcomes each quarter and each year.

Team Discussion

When you initiate a conversation with your employees and team(s), you could use some version of the following questions.

- How do we develop your organizational goals and strategies?

- How do we prioritize the highest-leverage projects that will lead to the desired outcomes each quarter and each year

Benchmarks

Next, we move into the benchmarks for this skill set.

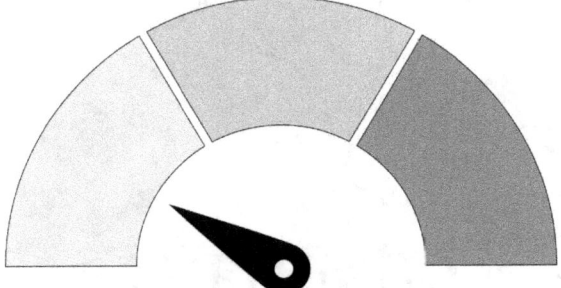

ORGANIZATIONAL STEERING LOWER RANGE

A leader and a team functioning in the lower range of proficiency in this skill set might describe it this way.

We set goals for each year along with an annual budget and ask our managers / teams to work toward those goals. We do not currently use any sophisticated planning methods beyond the basics.

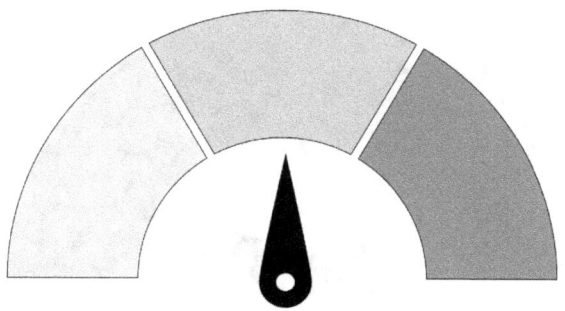

ORGANIZATIONAL STEERING
INTERMEDIATE RANGE

A leader and a team functioning in the middle range of proficiency in this skill set might describe it this way:

At the beginning of each calendar year, we decide on annual objectives and select key initiatives to support them. We check in on the progress toward those annual goals quarterly with our team. We do not currently use a specific tool or methodology to identify the highest leverage opportunities and projects, rather, we leave it up to our managers to figure out the best way to achieve the milestones. At the end of each year, we evaluate how we did and set new goals for the next year.

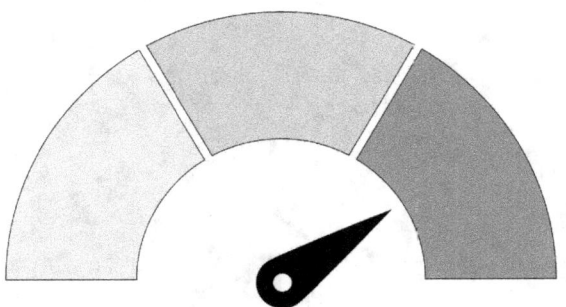

ORGANIZATIONAL STEERING HIGHER RANGE

A leader and a team functioning in the higher range of proficiency in this skill set might describe it this way.

We have a fairly sophisticated planning methodology for developing strategy and determining the best high-leverage annual initiatives and quarterly objectives. We update our annual plan, initiatives and priorities at least quarterly. We link our strategic plan to the high-leverage projects our managers and teams are implementing so that operations stay closely connected to our dynamically updated strategic plan.

Strategic Thinking and Planning

In this section, we zoom into the skill set we refer to as "Dynamic Steering." As the above definition and benchmarks indicated, as a review, this skillset concerns your organization's capacity to develop winning strategies, create annual goals, and select the highest leverage annual initiatives and quarterly projects that efficiently implement the strategy so that the organization can consistently hit its objectives. Different management and leadership experts may call this skill goal-setting, strategic planning, annual planning, quarterly planning, course correction, and dynamic steering.

Organizations that are effective at planning and organizational steering decide on annual objectives and select key initiatives to support them at the beginning of each calendar year; they then check in on the progress towards those goals throughout the year. While some organizations leave it up to the managers to figure out the best way to achieve the quarterly milestones on the annual plan, it is best to use a common tool or methodology to identify the highest leverage opportunities and projects each quarter.

Strategic Thinking vs. Strategic Planning

As effective organizational leaders, we need to be more precise when we use the terms strategic thinking, strategy, and the broader term "planning." Strategic thinking is not strategic planning. As strategy author Henry Mintzberg points out, one is synthesis; the other is analysis.

> *"Strategic planning is not strategic thinking. Indeed, strategic planning often spoils strategic thinking, causing managers to confuse real vision with the manipulation of numbers."*
> *– Henry Mintzberg*

This lesson will zero in on the specific skill called "strategic thinking." The product of strategic thinking" is called strategy. Let's zoom in on this concept called strategy.

> *Strategy without tactics is the slowest route to victory. Tactics without strategy is the noise before defeat.*
> *– Sun Tzu, The Art of War*

Many organizations throw the word "strategy" around liberally. They form task forces, hire consultants, and write extensive plans. Yet statistics show that most organizations fail to implement the plans they have spent so much time, effort, and money creating.

Why can only one in ten companies sustain growth and above-average returns for more than a few years?

"The fault does not lie with bad management, " says Harvard Business Professor Clayton Christensen, "unless you believe the management talent pool is like some perverse Lake Wobegon where 90 percent of managers are below average".

Christensen says the odds of lasting success remain "frighteningly low" because business people make decisions based on inadequate thinking.

When they see other companies achieving success, they try to put in place whatever "best practices" were part of that success story. The problem is not that lessons from top achievers, "habits of greatness," or any other collections of best practices are wrong—the problem is that they are right only some of the time, and only for some organizations, and only in some circumstances.

Learning to pay attention to specific circumstances is the essence of strategic thinking, which leads to developing more appropriate strategies because, as Christensen says, "things get predictable."

This section focuses on the essential elements of creating that predictability that leads growth companies consistently to success.

Some Helpful Definitions

A strategy is a set of actions, in a specific sequence, designed to achieve a desired outcome with minimum effort and cost, maximum benefit, and the highest probability of success.

We can define "strategic thinking" as the process by which the leadership of an organization envisions the organization's future and defines the critical assumptions, factors, and business philosophies necessary to achieve it.

To add some additional nuance, we can say that strategic thinking considers all the factors that can affect the success or failure of a company, department, or team.

Strategic thinking involves the deliberate and careful anticipation of and examination of vulnerabilities, threats, and opportunities.

I'm sure you are familiar with a SWOT analysis. As you undoubtedly know, SWOT is an acronym for Strengths, Weaknesses, Opportunities, and Threats. It's a basic yet certainly useful tool. It is one of the first tools many leaders use to begin to practice their strategic thinking skills.

Many organizations have adopted a tool referred to as a PESTLE analysis to get a more granular view of the circumstances a business is facing, including the broader industry and macroeconomic environment. Another acronym, of course, is PESTLE, which stands for Political, Economic, Social, Technological, Legal, and Environmental factors.

You might say that strategic thinkers who are elevating their skills often graduate from using SWOT to using PESTLE. The analyzing and strategizing inherent in what we are calling strategic thinking ultimately results in new ideas, goals, plans that will help the organization thrive in a competitive environment.

As we will see in this lesson, strategic thinking requires creativity, analysis, problem-solving, and communication skills. Strategic thinking skills include any skills that enable you to use critical thinking to solve complex problems and plan for the future.

Further Differentiating Strategic Thinking from Strategic Planning

Strategic planning focuses on analysis: breaking down a goal into steps, then formalizing those steps into plans that can be articulated, delegated, and executed. Strategic thinking produces strategic insights. It is creative and inductive in nature. Planning is more deductive. It is about breaking a goal down into smaller chunks and creating an action plan or project plan to "execute" the plan successfully. Planning benefits from a disciplined, linear, predictable, and repeatable methodology.

In this section, we will zoom in on strategic thinking skills that require intuition, creativity, and synthesis.

Strategic thinking results in a more comprehensive, complex, and integrated perspective on an organization and the challenges and obstacles it faces.

First used in a military context, the word strategy comes from the Greek word for "office of the general."

Historically, this occurred whenever a small army defeated a larger, better-resourced enemy.

In essence, strategy is about cleverly leveraging limited resources that result in non-linear performance gains.

It now has many connotations, including planning and deploying large-scale operations, using clever and resourceful methods in business, games, or war, and a maneuver designed to outsmart a competitor.

Put even more succinctly, strategy involves finding and using leverage.

Like any other complex skill, strategic thinking is best learned through practice, but many leaders do not have the opportunity or make the time to think strategically and accumulate the practice needed to develop this cognitive skill to the extent needed to be effective as organizational leadership, especially senior leaders (directors, vice presidents, and the C-Suite).

This section introduces some of the fundamental concepts of strategic thinking, highlights key thought leaders' perspectives on the subject, and provides guidelines organizational leaders can use to cultivate this capacity in themselves and their teams. This section highlights some of the key insights from two well-known experts, and you could even say "legends" in the field of strategic thinking: Michael Porter and Clayton Christensen.

In Michael Porter's classic Harvard Business Review article entitled, "What Is Strategy?" he draws key distinctions between what strategy is and is not. If you are a student of strategy or have read his work, you know that, according to Porter, if you aren't making any tradeoffs, then you don't actually have a strategy.

In another HBR classic entitled *"Making Strategy: Learning by Doing,"* Clayton Christensen outlines a three-stage model for developing successful strategies and points to the need for a deliberate mechanism through which resources are linked and aligned with the strategies. A key focus of Christensen's recommendations is to understand what he calls the "driving forces" impacting your organization.

In his classic Harvard Business Review article "*What Is Strategy?*" Porter points out that positioning, once the keystone of strategy, is now easily copied. He notes that many leaders fail to distinguish between operational effectiveness and strategy, both of which are essential for sustained success. "A company can outperform its rivals only if it can establish a difference it can preserve," Porter writes.

Understanding Strategic Fit

Strategic fit is the alignment of operational effectiveness with strategy. To support its strategy, a company should precisely link and align every key aspect of its operations—production, sales, delivery, and customer service. Harvard professor Clayton Christensen's work pioneered many aspects of business strategy and innovation, including the well-known concepts of the "S-Curve" and disruptive innovation.

His HBR article "*Making Strategy: Learning by Doing*" remains a classic analysis for intermediate to advanced students of strategic thinking. In it, he points out that strategic thinking is not a core competency in most companies, and he outlines two challenges that leaders face in developing and implementing a successful strategy.

First, leaders must ensure that the strategy does not reflect the biases of the management team that are often rooted in the organization's past successes. Second, leaders must ensure that once a viable strategy has been chosen, resources are allocated in a way that accurately reflects the strategy.

Christensen's research shows that such alignment rarely occurs, indicating the need for strategic thinking and planning methodology that can give leaders a systematic way to not only develop, but also to implement successful strategies.

Why is Strategic Thinking Essential

Your company is affected by the changing competitive landscape. You may need to be able to capitalize on new trends quickly, or you could fall behind. You will be more adept at anticipating, forecasting, and capitalizing on opportunities if you incorporate strategic thinking into your daily life and work routines as an organizational leader.

Strategic thinking allows you to be more effective in your role as a senior leader and make more contributions to your organization over time.

As suggested previously leadership teams frequently report that their executives and managers don't think strategically enough.

A common objective of managers' development plans is to learn to "think more strategically." But it is often the case that it is unclear what that actually looks like and how to learn to improve this skill.

This Is What Strategic Executives Do

They lift their head above day-to-day work and view the organization with a big-picture perspective.

They ask questions and challenge assumptions about the organization and the environment in which it operates. They gather data and interpret it

They use analysis tools and processes to evaluate options and make better choices that are more likely to lead to desired organizational outcomes.

Strategic Thinking Skills

Leaders are expected to think strategically. Every week you make decisions that help or, in some cases, hinder your team and your organization's ability to achieve its objectives.

Each decision you make has numerous implications as a manager... you have to work with the constraint that the information you have is limited and is often not comprehensive or complete, as well as the fact that many of the strategic decisions you need to make involve numerous variables.

Much of your success in your role rests on your ability to think strategically.

In this section we will cover some of the fundamentals of strategic thinking so that you can evaluate your proficiency in this essential ability, refine your understanding of the critical components and steps in the process, and discover ways that you can engage in strategic thinking as a practice so that you can get better at this essential skill quarter after quarter, year after year in your role as a senior executive.

One of the challenges of executive leadership is that there is a limited amount of information about the numerous internal and external forces influencing your organization.

Strategic thinking helps you evaluate options and develop effective strategies, which we can also call approaches, despite limited information about key variables.

In its most basic sense, strategic thinking is about analyzing opportunities and problems from a broad perspective and identifying ways to achieve greater leverage, defined as less effort or resources and more positive outcomes.

When you and the other leaders you work with think strategically, you can benefit the organization in several important ways. Your choices and direction are more likely to align with your overall business strategy.

You are able to find and implement more leverage, which improves your organizational performance and business results, and

You foster a culture that questions assumptions and encourages innovative thinking.

> *"Strategy-making is an immensely complex process involving the most sophisticated, subtle, and at times subconscious of human cognitive and social processes."*
> - Henry Mintzberg

Strategic thinking skills are any set of skills that enable you to solve complex problems and plan for the future using critical thinking. These include your sensemaking skills, your problem-solving skills, and your communication skills.

Strategic planning is frequently used to solve problems or address challenges, such as missed financial targets, inefficient workflows, or facing an emerging competitor. To implement a strategy addressing your primary challenge, you must first understand the problem and potential solutions. You can then devise a strategy to solve the problem.

In order to develop a strategy that will help your organization achieve its goals, you must be able to analyze a wide range of inputs, including financial statements and key performance indicators (KPIs), market conditions, emerging business trends, and internal resource allocation.

This preliminary sensemaking is critical for developing a strategy that is in line with your organization's current reality. Sensemaking is the subject of several lessons in this course.

Developing a strategy for your company, regardless of size, necessitates strong communication skills. Strategic thinking requires the ability to communicate complex ideas, collaborate with internal and external stakeholders, build consensus, and ensure everyone is aligned and working toward common goals.

What Does It Look Like?

Let's begin with the question, "What does it look like when a leader is thinking strategically?"

Leaders who are viewed as strategic thinkers exhibit some specific observable behaviors. These include:

-> They ask insightful and provocative questions and challenge assumptions

-> They maintain awareness and appreciation of the overall business strategy They focus on the future

-> They identify key issues and driving forces that positively or negatively impact the organization.

-> They maintain an open mind and actively seek out and hear alternative and opposing assumptions and views.

-> They demonstrate the ability to grasp abstract ideas and put the pieces together to form a coherent picture.

-> They are able to generate a wide range of options and visualize new possibilities.

-> They understand the cause-and-effect links between different elements of the system and how those come together to impact the team or organizational results.

It is useful to regard strategic thinking as a process that includes several specific, discrete cognitive activities. When you engage in this activity, you identify and analyze:

-> vulnerabilities and threats

-> opportunity costs associated with each move you are considering feasibility of each idea

-> risks associated with the actions you are considering taking the likelihood that various tactics will be effective the methods of aligning objectives with the overall plan

-> how your intended plans may be affected by the actions of customers, competitors, or suppliers, or customers.
As mentioned previously, an essential aspect of strategic thinking is to anticipate potential threats or problems so that you can mitigate or avoid them. As you uncover potential obstacles during the strategic thinking process, you will address them by:

-> Gathering relevant information about the problem

-> Clearly defining the threat or problem from a strategic point of view

-> Brainstorming possible solutions

-> Delegating assignments to key teams or members

-> Considering further downstream challenges those teams may need to confront and how to mitigate, avoid or overcome them.

"In strategy, it is important to see distant things as if they were close, and to take a distanced view of close things."
- Miyamoto Musashi, one of the greatest Samurais who ever lived

The Strategic Thinking Process

In the most simple terms, strategic thinking and/or planning consists of identifying and clarifying where we are now, where we want to be; and how we will get there. Naturally, we can break that into any number of steps, and different strategic thinking books and frameworks have different names for these phases or steps.

This section offers a useful framework with six distinct phases or steps. You are already doing some version of this. The idea is to get better at each aspect of strategic thinking. In later lessons in this course, we will unpack each of these and offer additional techniques and tools that enhance your ability to engage in these activities in your leadership role.

Six Steps for Strategic Thinking

1. *Zoom Out* - Zoom out to see the big picture

2. *Objectives* - Make objectives explicit Drivers - Identify key drivers

3. *Alternatives* - Generate alternatives or options for consideration

4. *Prioritize* - Clarify your priorities and the tradeoffs you intend to make

5. *Socialize* - Articulate your strategy and "socialize" it so that other stakeholders can support (or give you needed input as to why they are not in support)

Ways to Improve Your Strategic Thinking Skills

Following are specific things you can do to improve your strategic thinking skills over time:

Reflection - Set aside time to reflect and plan for the future, identify trends, prioritize tasks, and determine where to allocate resources

Biases - Uncover your own biases, so you can think more clearly about strategy

Better Data - Listen to your organization's subject matter experts and opinion leaders to obtain higher-quality information that you can use in your strategic thinking. Interview leaders from other functional areas (such IT, HR, R&D, marketing, or sales) to hear and understand different perspectives on the business.

Questions - Learn to ask great questions to uncover better options and plans. Examples of good questions include "Is this idea from a credible source?" and "Is this idea logical?" "Will this work in our specific circumstances?"

Consequences - Explore the downstream consequences of different strategies and directions. Playing devil's advocate with your ideas can allow you to preemptively identify weaknesses in your argument and equip you to defend your strategy when others ask questions.

Practice - As with any skill, you'll improve at strategic thinking the more you practice it and the more experience you gain.

It's definitely worth the time and effort. In truth, strategic thinking is one of the main things that distinguishes mediocre executives from outstanding executives

In this section, I defined strategy, strategic thinking, strategic fit. I described the observable behaviors of executives who are thinking strategically. I offered a six-step process for strategic thinking, and we offered six specific ways you can increase your strategic thinking skills.

Setting Priorities According to Leverage

One of the most important things a leader can do to have more influence on their organization and to have a greater positive impact on the organization is to set priorities based on leverage. In most basic terms, leverage is when you use a method to achieve greater output with less input. Leverage, then, is a function of "effort" and "output." We can also say, "effort" and "impact."

Clearly, in your organization there are many different needs, challenges and opportunities. Depending on the current landscape and context, the state of affairs of the internal environment as well as the macro environment in which the organization operates in, some activities, efforts, initiatives, projects, endeavors will have great impact on the organization's ability to achieve its goals. Similarly, certain undertakings, while they might require an enormous effort or investment, may yield only small gains in terms of benefit of positive impact.

Pareto's law suggests that about 80% of the results come from about 20% of the activities. The question I always ask leaders is this: Do you know your 20% this year and this quarter?

If you don't then you are not being a strategic leader. If you are unaware of which efforts, initiatives, investments and projects offer you the most benefit with the lowest cost/effort, then you are not being a good steward of the organization's resources. If you don't take the time to do the necessary analysis to assess and judge which efforts bring the most impact (with the least effort), then you are wasting your organization's resources. You are also wasting your time and energy and risking your leadership credibility. Credible leaders get results. Their strategies and plans achieve the outcome in a reasonable amount of time with a reasonable amount of resources.

Hopefully I am impressing upon you how critically important it is that you as a leader identify how your given goals, projects, initiatives, investments and undertakings stack up against the two poles of "effort / cost" and "benefit / impact" (value to the organization this year and this quarter).

The moral of this story is to find the leverage! There is no faster method I have found to find the leverage than the method I explain on the following pages.

To help leaders do this relatively easily and efficiently, I teach them the skill of "prioritizing." Strategic "prioritization" is central to effective strategic thinking and planning. And to be seen as a credible leader in the eyes of intelligent followers, the leader must have logical reasoning for prioritizing this effort (initiative or project) of that one.

To help leaders practice the skill of strategic prioritization, I provide a tool that I call a "Prioritization Matrix." As we will see shortly, this Prioritization Matrix tool is made up of two distinct concepts:

1. The relative effort or cost it will take to pursue an opportunity or execute a project or initiative; and

2. The relative strategic value of an opportunity or project (the benefit of the impact).

Estimating Effort and Cost

Estimating the bandwidth (effort) and the budget (cost) of a given opportunity or project is not easy. It is essential to take into consideration not only the tangible dimensions of the cost (cash, hours, bandwidth) but also the intangible dimensions. For example, the manager's focus and attention, the amount of energy it will take, stress level and emotional bandwidth to solve challenging personnel problems.

Effort and cost may also be influenced by timing, risk, and other factors, especially the broader team's skills and capacities for working on the business.

Estimating Relative Strategic Value

Now we will drill down into the "relative strategic value" or perceived impact of a given opportunity or project. Clearly not all priorities (projects, opportunities, goals, investments) offer the same value to the organization in a given year or quarter.

The value of an opportunity or project is largely a matter of fit with organizational strategy and goals for that year. Strategic value is also relative to the other opportunities and projects the organization is pursuing this year (and quarter). Many other factors play a role, including current company size, stage of growth, and market circumstances in a given year (and quarter).

Effectively estimating the relative strategic value (impact) of a given opportunity, project, or initiative of any kind requires a solid understanding of the organization's stage of growth, current needs, current opportunities and threats, problems, and so on.

No single person has the "correct answer" to how valuable an opportunity or project is. Each person on the management team (and involved in the project) will have their own assumptions and certain biases that come with the role and their past experience.

Different team members bring different vantage points, expertise, and data to the conversation. Each person's perspective can inform the "relative strategic value" this opportunity or project brings to the organization.

By assessing relative strategic value (low to high) on one axis and the effort and/or cost on the other axis, opportunities and projects can be positioned visually on an x-y matrix.

By plotting relative strategic value (impact) on one axis and "effort and cost" on the other, it produces a matrix with four quadrants. This becomes a very powerful strategic planning, prioritizing, strategic decision-making and organizational alignment tool.

I label each of these quadrants with *low* or *high* impact and *low* or *high* effort (includes cost).

And we can provide additional descriptive labels for these quadrants: *Delay, Work In, Selectively Invest,* and *Highest Leverage.*

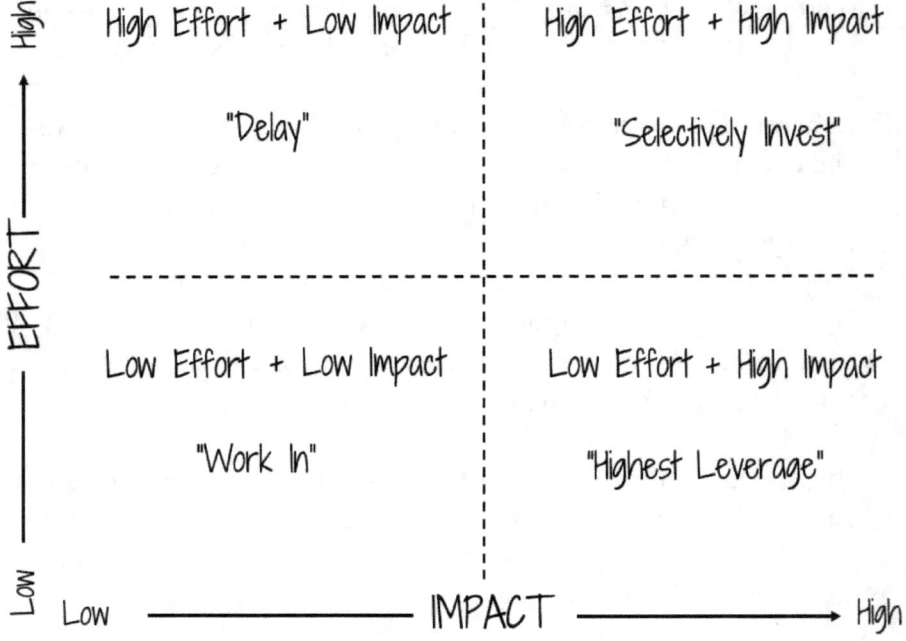

The first quadrant we will look at is described as *high* effort and low *impact*. We see it in the upper-left. We label this region of the matrix "Delay" because these opportunities and projects have very low leverage. Some leaders think of these priorities as "Good idea, but not enough resources." The delay region is where promising opportunities can wait "on deck" until next quarter or later when an easier way is found to do them or if business circumstances change and make them more valuable.

The *"Delay"* region is used to highlight opportunities and projects that leaders have decided will not create value this quarter or might distract the organization from things that are more important. This Delay area represents opportunities and projects that we are not going to put any energy, time or money into this quarter.

The choice to delay these opportunities and projects aligns with the strategic choices the organization has made. (For example, not pursuing a low-value customer segment even though the sales team wants to find revenue anywhere it can).

The next region is described as *low* effort combined with *low* impact seen in the lower-left. We label this region *"Work In"* because the opportunities and projects can be worked in occasionally when they are convenient, such as during slow times or when additional resources become available unexpectedly.

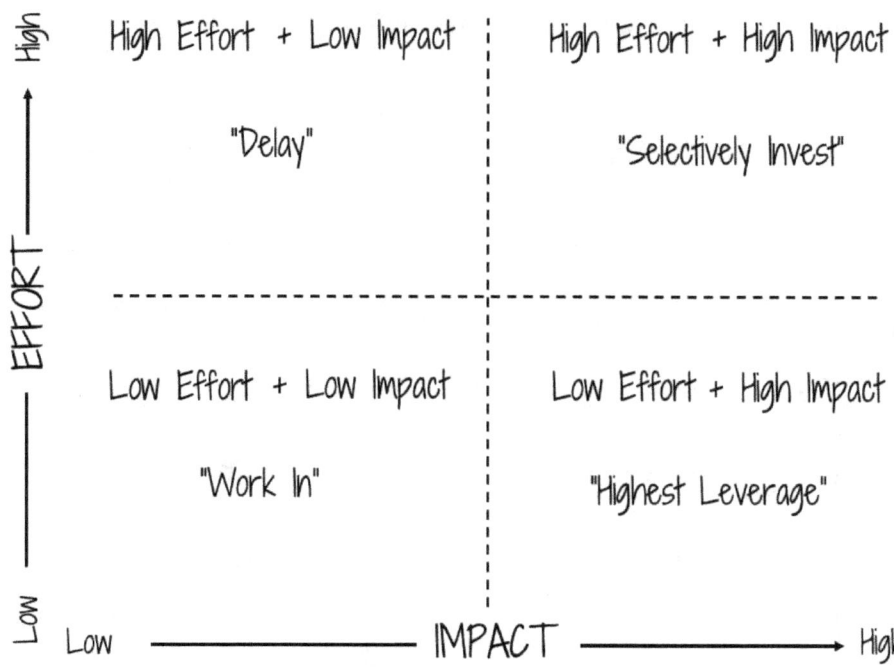

However, these opportunities and projects should never be pursued at the expense of higher-leverage projects.

The next section of the matrix is described as high impact and high effort. We see it in the upper-right. We label this region *"Selectively Invest"* because while these opportunities and projects are highly valuable, they are also very expensive or difficult to accomplish. Organizations have limited budget and bandwidth. It stands to reason that a given organization can and should only pursue a few of these large initiatives in a given calendar year.

Depending on the scope of these projects and the resources of the organization, this usually is limited to just 3-6 major initiatives each year. These difficult yet important initiatives should be considered and selected very carefully at the beginning of each calendar year and updated quarterly as circumstances change.

The next region is, by definition, high impact combined with low effort.

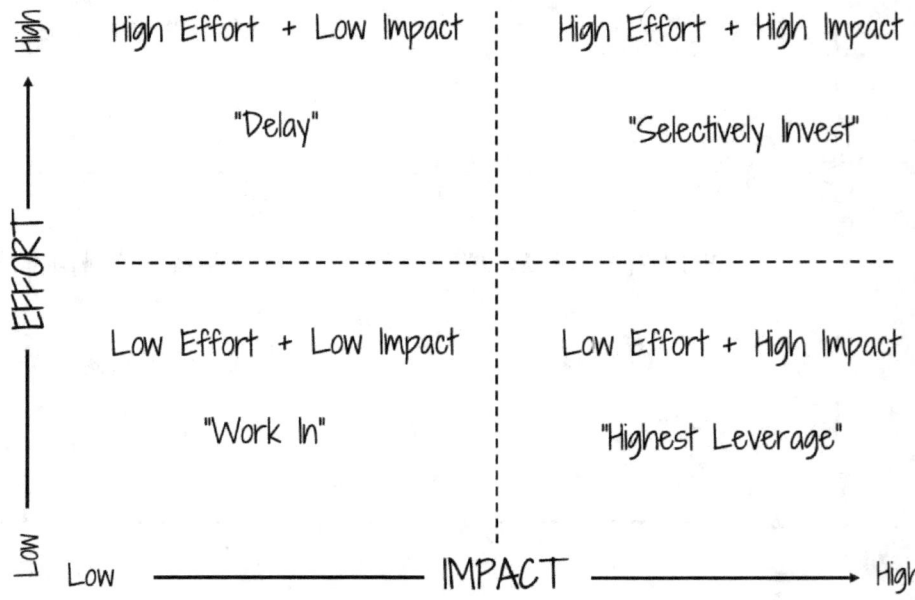

We see it in the lower-right quadrant. You can think of this lower-right quadrant as "low hanging fruit." Not only is it low hanging, meaning easily within reach, in this example the fruit is ripe and valuable (because it's on the high impact side of our diagram).

Clearly this is the region that represents the highest leverage in a given quarter. It is labeled accordingly as *Highest Leverage*.

If you are familiar with Pareto's Law that suggests 80% of your results come from 20% of your activities, then you will recognize this region as your highest leverage opportunities and projects

The activities, goals, initiatives, projects, efforts and investments in the "Highest Leverage" dimension are your "Pareto's 20%." Naturally you should try to do these projects first each quarter as they give you the biggest "bang for your buck."

Populating the Prioritization Matrix

Managers with different perspectives are often at odds about how much impact a given project will have on the organization. Put another way, they disagree about how valuable an effort / initiative / project is (how much organizational impact it will bring).

People are fond of their own ideas and pet projects and tend to over-value them. As a result, when management teams first populate the matrix with their lists of ideas and projects, nearly everything gets placed in the high-value regions.

Using this tool effectively requires open dialogue along with a willingness to question and test assumptions. Many ideas have merit but, because of cost or timing issues, simply should not be pursued in a given quarter. Teams also have difficulty accurately estimating the effort/cost required to take a project from concept to completion.

Over time, a more realistic assessment of organizational capacity is developed, and people tend to be more disciplined about where they place projects along the low to high effort and cost continuum.

Business circumstances are constantly changing. Some projects become more valuable over several months. Perhaps an easier or cheaper method is discovered to accomplish a project from one quarter to the next.

It is important to realize that the Prioritization Matrix is not a static, once-per-year tool. Rather, it is a dynamic map that must be continually updated (quarterly at a minimum or even monthly) in order to make sure that the map reflects the "territory".

Prioritization Matrix Pro Tips

Tip 1: The Prioritization Matrix is always for a calendar year and is updated quarterly.

Tip 2: The Selectively Invest projects will take two or more quarters to complete (perhaps all year).

Tip 3: The Highest Leverage projects should be framed so that they can be completed this quarter.

Tip 4: The Relative Strategic Value, labeled "Impact," is based on how valuable this opportunity or project is to the annual vision and strategy for the organization this calendar year.

Tip 5: Ask, "Is this project essential to us achieving our goals this year?" If yes, then it would be higher impact. If no, it would be lower impact.

Tip 6: Effort / Cost is based on bandwidth (time, energy, psychic bandwidth) and budget (financial investment required).

Tip 7: Ask, "How much effort in terms of labor, time, bandwidth, creativity, or emotional energy is required?"

And ask, "What is the cost associated with this opportunity or project?"

Tip 8: Remember, the Effort and Cost is "relative" to all the other opportunities and projects the organization is pursuing this year and quarter.

Tip 9: Relative strategic value (what we refer to as Impact for short) and relative effort and cost often changes mid-quarter as business circumstances evolve. When we hire new staff, it may be relatively speaking, easier to complete a project. Or if there is a competitive issue in the marketplace that must be addressed, then a project might have greater perceived impact in a given quarter.

In conclusion, remember that strategic thinking and planning is a complex skill that can't be learned, much less mastered in a short period of time.

This Prioritization Matrix is a crucial tool for managers to exercise their strategic thinking and planning skills with other managers in their current and ever-evolving business context. As you build out and then update your Prioritization Matrix each quarter (and review it frequently), you will have an opportunity to test your assumptions and discuss your priorities with other managers in real time. You can expect to become more skillful using this tool every quarter as you evaluate, iterate and implement the opportunities and projects that populate your matrix. See this tool as a piece of exercise equipment that helps you and your team strengthen your skill at "strategic prioritization" which is a subset of the skill we call "strategic thinking and planning," which in turn strengthens the skill set we call "organizational steering."

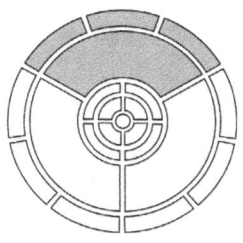

CONCLUSION: WHERE TO GO FROM HERE ON YOUR LEADERSHIP JOURNEY

Congratulations on completing this book. . Research studies suggest that less than 50% of non-fiction book buyers actually finish the books they buy. Thank you for your determination to complete this one. Now that you have read this book, you have a strong familiarity with the fundamental leadership abilities and the nine leadership core competencies. You have also learned about numerous frameworks, tools and techniques that fall under the three skill sets we see in this *Strategy & Alignment* dimension of leadership. While this is a very positive development, knowledge is not the same as skill. A skill is a "practice" that has been engaged until it becomes a habit.

If you want to improve your leadership, then must practice the techniques in this book. Developing the requisite skills described in this book will increase your competency in each of these dimensions. At minimum, you need to adopt and practice these techniques yourself. Experience shows that if you share some of these techniques with your team and invite them to practice these methods with you, as a team, you will learn them faster and your team will benefit from more than one person engaging in it.

Socializing these methods (techniques, behaviors) with your team will multiply the benefits for them.

As we learned in the discussion about "deliberate practice," practice doesn't make perfect, rather, perfect practice makes perfect. To increase your competency in these skill sets you have learned about, you must practice the techniques for many weeks (or months). This is the only way to learn a complex skill. You can't learn basketball from a book. You can't learn leadership from a book. But you can learn what you need to do in order to learn these techniques. We have used this method for 20 years helping leaders adopt new skills rapidly with consistent results. You can get the same results if you engage the practices described in this book.

I want to offer you a quick refresher about the principles of deliberate practice that are useful as implement this Practice-based Leadership Development methodology.

1) *Train technique* - To learn a complex skill, you must isolate the technique or skill, set specific goals based on best practices and benchmarks, practice with full attention and push beyond your comfort zone. You now know how to train.

2) *Rich feedback to calibrate and improve* - This involves practicing the techniques with full attention and effort, and obtaining immediate feedback to be able to calibrate and fine tune the new technique. One way to do this is to share the techniques and practices with your teammates so that they can give you feedback. The best feedback comes from people who have the skill. So if you have the opportunity to work with coaches or trainers who are familiar with these techniques, that will be ideal. This leads to the next key.

3) *You must get expert mentorship* – I have been able to provide an initial level of mentorship by describing these techniques. That is

an excellent start, and if you are very disciplined and diligent in practicing the methods as described, you can make some progress. However, mastery of these techniques, especially the more complex ones, requires getting individualized feedback and coaching from people who have legitimate expertise (who are experts in the specific techniques). Some of your coaches, advisors or trainers may be legitimate experts in one or more of these techniques (sensemaking, stakeholder alignment, organizational steering). Take advantage of that.

Here's how to apply this knowledge to your situation:

1. Assess your current leadership approach – Identify your dominant leadership style and evaluate where you need to expand your versatility.
2. Develop your leadership skills deliberately – Focus on practicing specific leadership techniques using the deliberate practice framework outlined in this book.
3. Adapt to different followers and contexts – Use the Leadership Rosetta Stone to recognize the worldviews of those you lead and adjust your leadership approach accordingly.
4. Commit to ongoing growth – Leadership is not a one-time event; it is a continuous process of learning, refining, and improving.
5. Attend a course or coaching program where you can receive expert guidance and ongoing feedback to help you internalize the skills efficiently.

To increase your competency in these skill sets you have learned about, you must practice the techniques for many weeks (or months). This is the only way to learn a complex skill. To put this method into practice, active and ongoing training in the specific techniques is required. That is best done in a training and/or coaching environment. My partners and I, across numerous institutes and academies, offer numerous Integral Leadership training and coaching programs in various formats and at various price points to be able to accommodate most leaders in most circumstances. If you are serious about becoming a more effective leader, or if you support leaders (as a trainer or coach), I hope that you will pick up and read one or more of my other (longer, more detailed) books on this subject. You can find all of my books on Amazon.com. I also hope you will consider joining one of the many Integral Leadership training and coaching programs that my partners and I offer. My fourteen books are used as textbooks at multiple institutions and academies and offer various versions of my Integral Leadership training by several different names, including the Integral Leadership Program (many versions across several academies), the Integral Leadership MBA, the Executive Leadership Program and the C-Suite Leadership Program. When you participate in an in-depth online or in-person training based on this content, and especially if you obtain group or one-on-one coaching from a coach who has been trained in my content, then you will be able to rapidly accelerate your development as a leader, and ultimately become the kind of respected influential, impactful, successful leader you know that you are destined to be.

I look forward to continuing this "conversation" with you in one of my other books.

Brett Thomas

ABOUT THE AUTHOR

Leadership authority Brett Thomas is an expert on leadership development, integral theory, and developmental psychology. He has written 14 books on management and leadership. In collaboration with Ken Wilber, he created the world's first "unifying theory of leadership" and wove together 100 years of leadership theory into a unified model that explains which theories and approaches will work with which people and circumstances that also accurately predicts which leadership styles and approaches will be disastrous failures with which specific types of people and circumstances. He is the creator (along with his mentor Ken Wilber) of the popular practice known as Integral Leadership. Brett's fourteen books are used as textbooks around the world in many of the top leadership training and coaching programs. Numerous institutions and academies teach various versions of Brett's highly respected Integral Leadership Program, sometimes using other names such as the Executive Leadership Program, the C-Suite Leadership Program, and the Integral Leadership MBA. Brett is a serial entrepreneur and leader working behind the scenes in more than a dozen humanitarian efforts under the umbrella of the international non-profit (501c3) he quietly founded years ago. Brett is the mentor, advisor, and coach to hundreds of CEOs. Dozens of his clients have scaled their companies from tens of millions to hundreds of millions in revenue and even to over a billion in some cases (while going from dozens to hundreds to thousands of employees), always with a "balanced scorecard" and "triple bottom line," meaning a rich, healthy, beloved culture never merely profit-seeking. In addition to writing books, Brett serves as an advisor to dozens of CEOs and C-Suite Executive Teams, serves as a fractional COO to several organizations, and teaches in several academies. In addition to co-founding two of the most respected and admired leadership academies in the world, he is also one of the primary co-founders of the Conscious Capitalism movement, which he helped launch nearly two decades ago to make "business a force for good."

OTHER BOOKS BY BRETT THOMAS

Integral Leadership: The World's First Unifying Theory of Leadership That Will Forever Change How You Understand, Practice and Develop Leadership

Blowing the Whistle on Bogus Leadership: Veteran Industry Insider Reveals Why the Leadership Development Industry is Not Developing Leaders.

The Leadership Rosetta Stone: Discover Which Leadership Approaches Will Work With Which People and Circumstances and Which Approaches Will Be Disastrous Failures with Which People and Circumstances

The Universal Leadership Model: Simplicity on the Other Side of Complexity

Accelerating Leadership: The Groundbreaking Method for Rapid Leadership Skill Development That Achieves Twice the Results in Half the Time at a Fraction of the Cost

Reinventing Leadership: Discover the Revolutionary Method That Thousands of Leaders and Organizations Are Using to Rapidly Improve Leadership Performance and Organizational Results

Teamwork & Culture: How the Most Successful Leaders Create the Container, Communicate Effectively, and Consistently Keep Everyone Engaged and Motivated

Execution & Performance: How the Most Successful Leaders Close Expectation Gaps, Maintain High Accountability and Productivity, and Reliably Deliver Excellent Results
Worldviews: The Four Mindsets That Determine What People Perceive, Believe and Value, and Which Leadership Styles They Will Follow

Leadership Styles: How to Be a More Respected, More Influential and More Impactful Leader Using the Right Leadership Style With the Right People and Circumstances

Leadership Intelligence: Learn How Your Cognitive, Emotional, Social and Moral Development is Impacting Your Leadership Performance and How Leaders Can Now Benchmark and Boost These Intelligences

Measuring Leadership: How to Diagnose, Develop and Deliver Outstanding Leadership Performance by Benchmarking the Three Abilities and Nine Core Competencies That Matter Most (To be published in 2025)

Academic Books:

Handbook of Leadership Development: The Definitive Guide for Executives in Charge of Leadership Development

Leadership Psychology: How to Apply Crucial Insights from Positive Psychology, Developmental Psychology, Integral Psychology and Organizational Psychology to Develop More Effective Leaders (To be published in 2025)

www.ingramcontent.com/pod-product-compliance
Lightning Source LLC
Chambersburg PA
CBHW052147220526
45471CB00004B/1569